SMALL-HEADED FL

Seen Yesterday.

He Didn't Leave His Name.

SMALL-HEADED FLYCATCHER.
Seen Yesterday.
He Didn't Leave His Name.
And Other Stories

Pete Dunne

Drawings by Louise Zemaitis

 UNIVERSITY OF TEXAS PRESS, AUSTIN

Requests for permission to reproduce material from this work
should be sent to Permissions, University of Texas Press, P.O.
Box 7819, Austin, TX 78713-7819.

⊗ The paper used in this publication meets the minimum
requirements of American National Standard for Information
Sciences—Permanence of Paper for Printed Library Materials,
ANSI Z39.48-1984.

LIBRARY OF CONGRESS
CATALOGING-IN-PUBLICATION DATA

Dunne, Pete, 1951–
[Essays. Selections]
Small-headed flycatcher ; Seen yesterday ; He didn't leave
his name : and other stories / Pete Dunne.
      p.   cm.
ISBN 0-292-71599-4 (cloth : alk. paper.) —
ISBN 0-292-71600-1 (paper : alk. paper)
1. Bird watching.   2. Birds.   I. Title.   II. Title: Seen
yesterday.   III. Title: He didn't leave his name.
QL677.5.D85   1998
598'.07'234—dc21   97-43354

To Beth Van Vleck,
who watches birds too.

CONTENTS

Part 4: . . . AND BIRDING

Part 5: REFLECTIONS

ACKNOWLEDGMENTS

Writers are helped by a support force whose ranks are filled by just about everyone they know. It includes coworkers whose concentration is habitually broken by queries like "Hey, does *Phragmites* have one *t* or two?"; friends whose calls to finalize dinner plans are considered invitations to use them as editorial sounding boards; dogs that wait by the back door until the urgency of their whining finally cuts through a writer's trance; and overnight delivery people who understand that an unanswered knock at the front door means go around to the back door, leave the envelope . . .

And let the dogs out.

Broad-based support (and broad-brush gratitude) notwithstanding, it is impossible *not* to single out a few individuals whose contribution during the working of these essays has earned them special thanks. These include editors Richard Roberts, Fletcher Roberts, Tim Gallagher, Victoria Irwin, Jane Crowley, and Eldon Greij, whose friendship and counsel are worth any writer's envy, as well as Sheila Lego, Marleen Murgitroid, and Beth Van Vleck, whose talents as proofreaders were gratefully accepted and are even more gratefully acknowledged.

Of course, nothing I attempt could come to fruition without the patient indulgence of my wife, Linda, or the support of the Cape May Bird Observatory staff.

PREFACE

"I guess I'll be a writer someday," I said in response to one of the stock questions asked of, and by, people who are destined to become friends. This assertion, uttered on the north lookout of Hawk Mountain Sanctuary in 1975, elicited no response from hawk counter Michael Heller. Only years later did Michael confess that he didn't place much stock in my disclosure at the time.

"Everybody," he recalls thinking, "thinks that they are going to be a writer someday."

Today Michael is a plantation manager with the Chesapeake Bay Foundation. I am the director of the New Jersey Audubon Society's Cape May Bird Observatory. But back in the winter of 1975–1976, when Michael and I enlivened evenings by knocking back dark beers and reading the passages of favorite authors to each other aloud, I was still searching for my niche and hoping that the hawk migration study I was going to conduct for the New Jersey Audubon Society come spring would lead to something . . .

A job. A career. Maybe even an avenue to express the cauldron of thoughts and observations that boiled inside me—and have since been forged into essays, stories, and articles:

In magazines like *Audubon, American Birds, Bird Watcher's Digest, Birder's World, Birding, Living Bird, Natural History, Nature Conservancy, New Jersey Audubon, WildBird, Wildlife Conservation.*

In the biweekly column I penned between 1986 and 1995 for the New Jersey Sunday section of the *New York Times,* titled "In the Natural State."

In the *Peregrine Observer,* the newsletter of Cape May Bird Observatory, which served as the first vehicle for my stories and from which the essays of my first book, *Tales of a Low-Rent Birder,* were drawn.

Followed by *Hawks in Flight,* followed by *More Tales of a Low-Rent Birder,* followed by *The Feather Quest, Before the Echo, The Wind Masters* . . .

And now this book.

Yes, I guess I became a writer—a pretty prolific one too, if the volume of essays discarded while selecting favorites for this collection is any measure. In fact, I do *so* much writing for *so* many publications that readers sometimes ask *how* I can I write so much and not go dry. There are three reasons, I think.

First and foremost, I really love watching birds and delight in sharing my passion with others, whether in the field or in print.

Second, the focus and tone of the columns I write are thematically apportioned so each is approached with a different mind-set. For example, essays written for "The Catbird Seat," my regular column in *Living Bird,* trade heavily upon the foibles of birders and birding. They are short, whimsical, and sassy. By comparison, essays drafted for "American Birding," the column I once penned for now defunct *American Birds,* tend to be longer, more situational, and more philosophical.

Articles drawn from my "Beak to Tale" column in *Wild Bird News* are terse and people-oriented. Those crafted for "Birder at Large," which appears in *Birder's World,* are nostalgic and focused primarily upon birds themselves.

So each column's essays have a different style, a different perspective (offering a refreshing difference for writer and reader alike).

And the final reason to account for how I can draw from the

writer's well so freely and not run dry? I'm half-Irish, genetically linked to the planet's greatest race of storytellers.

That's how.

You may be curious about the title: *Small-Headed Flycatcher. Seen Yesterday. He Didn't Leave His Name.* It is the title of the book's longest essay, but a piece distinguished more by origin than length. Unlike the other thirty-three essays in this collection, "Small-Headed Flycatcher" was initially crafted to be spoken, not read. The audience was the American Birding Association members on the occasion the association's 1992 convention in Mobile, Alabama.

I'm too sly a storyteller to steal my own thunder (meaning I'll not unravel the story line here), but, as readers must know, stories are not spun from thin air. Behind every story there lies another: the story of the story's crafting. So for readers who would like a peek behind the writer's slate, here is the story behind the story—the story behind the writing of "Small-Headed Flycatcher."

In 1991, one year before the ABA convention, I was asked to be the banquet speaker at the Texas Ornithological Society's annual dinner. The invitation was tendered by then president, and friend, Dr. Bill Graber—a straight-shooting, straight-talking Texas gentleman.

My program, an audiovisual-augmented accounting of the year of birding and travel that was the substance of my book *The Feather Quest,* went well. Later, over drinks, I asked Bill how he enjoyed the program, and in a Texas-tempered baritone he replied, "Why, Pete, that was a *fine* program. A *fine* program," which is, of course, precisely what a guest speaker wants to hear.

"You know," continued the person whose love of honest truth would have earned a handshake from Diogenes, "that was *almost* as good as a story I once heard Peter Matthiessen give to us, several years ago, about his rediscovering heath hens on some tiny island off the coast of Massachusetts . . .

"Now that," said my gracious, truth-loving host, "was a *fine* story."

No storyteller, not even one who appreciates truth, likes to be told (even when it is true) that *their* story isn't as good as somebody else's story. And while I am a frank admirer of Peter Matthiessen's writing, I felt brazenly confident that I could tell a better *story* than Peter Matthiessen because . . .

Because like I said, I'm Irish!

So picking up Bill Graber's unmindfully dropped gauntlet, I cold-bloodedly set out to craft a better birding story than the one spun by Peter Matthiessen, using, for comparison's sake, the same basic story line—the rediscovery of a bird believed to be extinct—but drawing from and weaving in a different set of historic events: those relating to the finding of a bird whose discovery was independently claimed by rival artists John James Audubon and Alexander Wilson.

I threw everything I had into it. Every storyteller's trick. Every wordsmithing skill. All the Irish that was honestly mine to draw upon and even a measure that was not, that came from some vast depth, beyond the reach of my skill.

And at one marvelous moment during that inaugural telling, before an audience of five hundred listeners, I held a pregnant pause to the painful limit and was rewarded by the gratifying sound of *silence*. Utter silence.

"Got you," I thought quietly to myself. And I did have them too, an audience empathetically bound to the teller by the telling—had them right to the story's uncertain end.

No storyteller hopes for or garners more.

It just so happened that my friend Bill Graber was reigning vice president of ABA at the time and presiding over the banquet. So after the program. After the applause. After all the well-wishers (and the gainsayers) had had their say, I sashayed over to Dr. Graber and asked (oh so very casually) what he thought of the program.

"*Pete,*" said the man who didn't have a shred of memory concerning our earlier conversation, "I've got to tell you, that was a *fine* story, a *fine* story."

"You know," he continued after a moment's thought, "*That* was *as good* a story as one I once heard Peter Matthiessen tell at a meeting of the Texas Ornithological Society about . . ."

So I guess what I'm telling you is that I tied.

I hope you enjoy "Small-Headed Flycatcher."

Pete Dunne
Cape May, New Jersey

SMALL-HEADED FLYCATCHER.
Seen Yesterday.
He Didn't Leave His Name.

Part 1

STORIES

ABOUT

FAMILY

GIFT OF SEED

The house smelled of turkey and echoed with the sound of grand-children. We opened arms and hugged.

"Hello, Dad," I said.

"Solstice cheer!" he exclaimed. "Hurry up. There's something I want to show you."

My father turned, and a grimace twisted the smile from his face. He started toward the glass doors that open onto the deck, and though his legs are long, his steps were pained and short—a result of the Lyme disease that had taken much of his agility and very nearly his life.

We gained the doors and, like a child peeking around the cor-ner on Christmas morning, he leaned forward, studied the bird feeders with binoculars, then relaxed.

"He's not there now," he whispered. "Wait."

We did wait. Father and son. Watching chickadees and spar-rows, waiting for the new bird that had joined the ranks of my fa-ther's feeder regulars.

I saw my mother in the kitchen, working her usual culinary magic. Our eyes met, and we exchanged greetings along visual pathways. In response to my cocked eyebrow, she nodded in the direction of the feeders and smiled.

It was good to see the smile. It had not been there the last time we'd been together.

"We have to find something to catch his interest," she had im-plored more than urged back in October. "He can't get around like he used to. He can't use his hands very well. If he just sits in a chair all day, we're going to lose him."

"What about putting up some bird feeders out back," I suggested. "A couple of tube feeders filled with sunflower seeds for chickadees and finches. A platform feeder with millet for sparrows. A thistle tube to keep the goldfinches fat and sassy and— maybe some suet. Mom, a feeding station offers more color than a fish tank and more action than a meat counter when ground beef goes on sale."

"It's perfect," I continued. "Hours of entertainment. You get to know all the regulars and itch for each new arrival. You cheer on the chickadees, laugh at the nuthatches, and chastise the evening grosbeaks for hogging all the sunflower seeds."

"Besides, if keeping Dad sharp is the key, wait till he tries matching wits with squirrels. It's easier to keep the kids out of your pies than to keep squirrels out of your feeders."

"All right," she agreed. "Let's try it." That was two months ago.

"It was here just a minute ago," my father promised. "It likes the thistle feeder," he added to hold my attention.

"There!" he shouted as a bird flew in, claiming a perch. "That's it! Is that a redpoll?"

"That's a common redpoll," I affirmed, studying the puffy ball of feathers with the crimson cap. "Great bird!"

When he turned in triumph, I saw that the smile was back on his face, and the gleam in his eyes would have rivaled that of any child in the room. To look at those eyes, you'd never guess they'd ever known pain.

BROTHER MIKE'S RETREAT
FROM BIRDING

You've never met my brother Mike. He's what you'd call normal. Wife, kids, house in the 'burbs. Plays a little golf. Watches football on the tube. Lives for his lawn.

You've never met my brother Mike—but you probably know people like him. So you'll understand why I was having such a tough time convincing him that birders are normal.

We were standing on the hawk watch platform at Cape May Point State Park. I was looking at hawks. Mike was looking at the hawk watchers.

"You mean people come and stand here of their own volition?" he whispered (not wanting to hurt anyone's feelings).

"Travel hundreds, even thousands, of mi . . . *Peregrine over the bunker!*" I yelled as one hundred pairs of binoculars swiveled with the precision of a parade ground maneuver.

"How'd you get them to do that?" he demanded. "It's like some kind of totalitarian cult ritual."

"Hardly," I replied. "Birders are pretty independent."

"I'll say," he said, looking down the ranks, taking in an assortment of outerwear that ranged from Abercrombie and Fitch fine to Salvation Army discard (but leaning heavily on the side of Salvation Army). That's when someone produced a road-killed Virginia rail and started passing it around. Mike didn't say a word, but his eyes, looking squarely into mine, spoke volumes.

I guess to people whose keenest ambition is a close-cropped lawn, the antics of birders must appear odd. Normal people work like crazy for the privilege of sleeping in on Saturday until after the sun stops casting shadows. Birders get up *before* the sun casts shadows.

Normal people find a bird dropping on the hood of their newly washed car and go ballistic. Birders look up to see what's nesting on the overhanging limbs.

In my efforts to paint a palatable picture of my avocation, I have avoided telling brother Mike about some of the more suspect adventures birding has led me to. I never told him about the midnight encounter on that elevated railway two miles out in a marsh. There wasn't enough room on the tracks for the train *and* the members of my Big Day birding team, so we, being gallant, elected to step into the marsh.

I never told him about the time Patty H. skidded to a halt on an iced-over and totally blind I-95 exit ramp to point out my life hawk owl, or the time Bob B. and I canoed an ice-choked Delaware River on the Walnut Valley Christmas Bird Count just to add bufflehead to the count.

"It's okay," I explained to the near apoplectic park service ranger who met us at the landing. "We didn't dump, and we only had to chop ourselves free twice."

I've never told Mike about winter pelagic trips—how people will pay money and throw up all day for the chance of seeing a great skua or about the liquid-purging walk down Sycamore Canyon whose prize is a drab-looking sparrow that defines its territory vertically.

And I certainly never told Mike about Attu. How could you hope to explain (to a normal person) why people are willing to pay the price of a luxury cruise to spend three weeks in a building that doesn't meet the federal government's minimum standards for a homeless shelter and brave weather conditions that would freeze an eider to see birds that don't belong there?

Or how it is perfectly normal for a student living on a budget that wouldn't sustain an anorexic cat to brandish fifteen-hundred-dollar binoculars.

Or why a doting, loving father will risk a daughter's heartbreak (and a wife's wrath) and get to the church (after the fact) convinced that getting the bird constitutes pragmatic absolution.

It was all I could do to explain why a bunch of people passing a dead bird around constituted normal behavior.

"It's an opportunity to study a rarely seen bird," I explained. "It's the same as keeping a collection of study skins but better, since the plumage is fresher."

"You people keep dead birds?" he asked.

"Just the skins," I explained. "Until we're ready to prepare them, we store them in the freezer."

"You keep dead birds in the freezer?" he asked, believing me even less.

"Sure," I said, discreetly avoiding mention of the dead otter that was also vying with the frozen vegetables for freezer space. "We've got permits. It's legal."

The fact that there were laws governing such behavior seemed to comfort Mike. If birding was regulated (like everything else), maybe birding was indeed normal.

That's when someone yelled "*Wheatear!*" and several hundred people stampeded to the far side of the parking lot, where they proceeded to clamber atop the roofs of cars (in some cases not their own). It was the only way to see the bird perched on the roof.

"Want to see it?" I asked (I encouraged).

"I don't think so," he replied.

"Well . . . I'll see you later," I said, edging away.

"Later," he affirmed, edging the other way.

The next time we saw each other was Christmas. The subject of birding never came up.

THE WISDOM OF SISTERS

"Peter! Come to the window. QUICK!" I took the steps two at a time, reaching the kitchen window at a speed commensurate with the urgency in my sister's voice.

"Look," she said, directing my attention toward the backyard. "A hawk or something and it's killing a bird." I followed the line drawn by her finger and absorbed the scene.

"Cooper's hawk," the analytical portion of my brain deduced. A superb predator. A cruise missile of a raptor that can move through woodlands like smoke and match the movement of fleeing prey the way a mirror mimics.

"And a starling," I added, studying the bird pinned to the lawn—waiting for and absorbing the jolt of pity that comes of witnessing another creature's demise.

"It's still alive," my sister shouted.

"Yes," I said.

We've got to do something," she declared, starting for the door.

"No," I said, not loudly but convincingly. My sister returned to the window, absorbed the scene again, then turned and put all her anguish into a question.

"Why?" she demanded of her older, bird-learned brother whose feeders had drawn both the bird that was pinned and the bird that pinned it. *Why* should we, as thinking, feeling creatures not impose ourselves between a predator and its prey? As the starling struggled and its life ebbed, I tried to formulate an answer that would do at least small justice to the truth.

I thought of telling my sister that predation is a natural process—one that unites two species in a ritual of recycling, where both are moved toward higher levels of evolutionary perfection.

I thought of telling her that nature is profligate—always creates more than she needs—and that Cooper's hawks are just nature's way of cleaning house.

I thought of inviting her to study the young hawk and see it with my eyes. A streak-breasted bird of the year. Thin, probably starving. Chances were it would die before spring. Most of the Cooper's hawks born in any given year do not live to maturity.

I even considered being flippant and obtuse, telling her that the hawk was just another bird coming to the feeder.

But I did none of these things. I simply told her the truth as I knew it.

"Because we have no standing," I said. "I don't like everything I see in nature, and I don't understand it either. But I'm not smart enough or wise enough to second-guess nature, so I don't."

I thought that this disclosure would be enough to stay my younger sister's compassionate impulses, but I was wrong.

"Well, I may not be as smart as you are and I may not know anything about birds, but I'm going to save that bird," she said, turning, running.

And she did too.

KALEIDOSCOPE EYES

Our car rolled to a stop in front of the copse of trees. Northwest winds whipped the outer leaves, giving branches the properties of tentacles.

"Ready?" I asked.

"In a minute," wife Linda insisted, barely keeping her exasperation in check.

It was Sunday and early. Tomorrow was Monday and a school day. The semester's first exam was imminent, and my sudden intrusion into what had promised to be a day of study had not been greeted enthusiastically. In fact, initial efforts to pry Linda from her desk—to show her "something incredible"—had met hard resistance.

But as respectful as I try to be of my spouse's time, *this* time "No" was not an acceptable answer. This time she had to come with me.

Because I had found something incredible that morning, you see. In the trees. At the end of an old road leading out onto open marsh. Something wide-eyed, marvelous, and heart-stoppingly beautiful.

It was a spectacle so spectacular that it stripped away adult reserve and made me gasp like a child. It was the perfect example of why, after forty-four years, I still reside in this overpopulated and environmentally stressed state and why I have no thought but to continue to do so.

It was imperative that Linda see this spectacle too. Why? Because eight years of residency has not been time enough to pry the horizon from Linda's mind. Her roots and standards are still set in the unencumbered riches of the American West. To her mind, every day she wakes in the East is a day that begins with compromise.

You cradle-to-grave easterners who have never lived anywhere else may be confounded, even affronted, by Linda's attitude. You may not understand how a woodland differs from a wilderness or why a person might prefer the latter.

Well, I understand a little, barely. I have felt the power of the Rockies—the mountain range whose afternoon shadow once fell on Linda's doorstep. I have floated in the self-dissolving calm of Prince William Sound—the body of water that Linda once called her playground.

I know how, after just a few days or weeks in places like these, human souls expand to encompass them and how returning to an environment where human activity patterns are plotted around peak traffic periods is stifling.

I can only guess how a person raised by the open standards of the West must feel when they move East. It has been eight years since Linda left Wyoming and moved to New Jersey. And while she no longer cries whenever our eastbound plane circles for a landing, her eyes, fused to the landscape below, are clouded with disquiet.

I'm different, of course. Born into compromise; a seeker of beauty when and wherever I can find it. There are many wonderful natural treasures housed in New Jersey. But you have to know how to find them.

I've tried to explain this to Linda. "Nature in New Jersey," I tutor, "is like the contemplation of a bonsai garden or peering into a kaleidoscope. Focus on the beauty in front of you; block out the world around you. That's the trick.

"Don't think like a westerner," I counsel. "You'll go crazy with loss. The eastern old-growth forests are cut and gone. The rivers are sullied. The cities and people are here for keeps. Forget these things.

"Think *small*," I counsel her. "Think eastern. When you see a stand of bloodroot blooming in the spring, absorb the wonder of it. When you round a corner and find a valley uncompromised by corporate headquarters, love it."

But I was brought up in New Jersey, and this discipline comes easy to me. Looking small and looking close and overlooking the things she does not care to see is something Linda does not do easily or well.

I recall a morning spent in the New Jersey highlands, on a marginally traveled highway named Clinton Road. We'd gone to look for northern breeding birds—warblers and vireos and thrushes whose songs fill Canadian zone woodlands.

It was in my estimate a terrific day, one filled with encounters. But over the course of the morning, Linda's enthusiasm ebbed, and silence closed around her like a shroud.

"What's the matter?" I finally asked.

"It doesn't even trouble you, does it?" she asked, gesturing toward the side of the road.

"What doesn't trouble me?" I asked, genuinely puzzled.

"That," she said, pointing directly at a pile of roadside trash—the cans, bottles, and product wrappings discarded by motorists. "That," she said, not even wanting to honor the stuff with a name.

I never even saw the trash. I was wearing my New Jersey blinders and had looked right past it.

Another time we were engaged in a Christmas bird count. Our territory in northern Morris County was a coveted patch—an overgrown gravel pit that habitually produced unusual birds for the count: assorted owls, lingering half-hearty songbirds, even a great egret on one momentous occasion, a first for the count.

As we picked our way through one of the trash heaps that abound in woodlands adjacent to heavily suburbanized areas, and as I stepped between sixty-gallon drums that may or may not have contained their original contents, I realized that Linda wasn't beside me anymore. I turned to find her on the far side of the dump, and she was crying angry tears.

"How can you stand to be here?" she wailed. And after she pointed it out, I found that she was right. I couldn't stand it either. We left, and since that morning in December we've never gone back.

We donned binoculars, got out of the car, and walked toward the trees. The grove was dome-shaped and hollow. Once there must have been a house within it, and the trees had served as a buffer against the winds that whipped across the open marsh.

But the house, even the foundation, was gone. Only the trees remained, and at the end of the road on that open marsh, they served as sanctuary to hosts of migrating things.

Even before stepping through the portal cut into living trees, even before the contents of the grove were unveiled to our eyes, we could see myriads of migrating birds. Redstarts fanned their tails in the leaves, and their wings flickered like flames. Black-and-white warblers moved along limbs like wind-up toys, and assorted flycatchers made acrobatic swoops through the foliage.

But it wasn't the birds I wanted Linda to see. It was something else, another migrant that had taken shelter in the grove. Covering the vegetation in blossomlike clusters were roosting monarch butterflies—hundreds of them. They made the branches bow beneath their weight. They carpeted the earth with cold, numbed bodies that came to life with the warmth of a hand.

Now that the sun had risen and warmed the interior of the grove, many of the insects had taken to the air. Avoiding the windy world beyond the trees, they swirled beneath the canopy.

Shards of sunlight falling through the leaves flickered and fled. Warblers and flycatchers darted and danced. And all around us, like bright orange leaves tumbling in a vortex, the monarchs swirled.

"It's like being inside a kaleidoscope," Linda breathed, taking my hand.

"Yes," I said. "That was my thought too."

Outside the grove there was another world and other people.

Outside the garden there were ugly things and discouraging things and painful things too.

But inside the grove there was beauty to rival the splendor of the Rocky Mountains and maybe Prince William Sound too. And for a little while, for lucky eyes that had been brought to see, there was wonder enough to fill even the most western soul.

THE BIRDIN' OF KINDNESS

I'm a reserved person—take pride in my ability to face disappointments stoically. But when I opened my third straight birthday card displaying an insipid cartoon canary and the announcement "A little bird told me it was your birthday," I put my face in my hands and wept.

It's not that I mind getting older. Heck, I've been doing that all my life. What vexes me is the unmindful cruelty of nonbirders. Ever since it became known that I'm a birder, nonbirding friends and relatives have been demonstrating their support by showering me with bird-related junk.

And I'm sick of it.

"Why another bird card?" I said to my open hands. "Why not a card depicting some incontinent old drooler welcoming me to the forties or some scantily clad vision promising earthly delights beyond the reach of my years?"

"*I'm normal!*" I wanted to scream. "*I pay taxes . . . cut the lawn . . . cheat on my diet, just like normal people!* Why don't I ever get anything but bird stuff?"

What is it about birdwatching that makes mothers think that the ugliest lamp in the history of porcelain will make a splendid gift so long as the lamp shade boasts an impossible assortment of tanagers, Old World buntings, and warblers standing in the snow? What is it about our avocation that turns tasteful, decor-sensitive people into the gift-buying equivalent of Roller Derby fans?

In anticipation of my upcoming birthday, I inventoried our living room and took stock of my unwanted stock, to make room for a new wave of kiln-fired kiwi toothpick holders, bluebird of happiness paperweights, music boxes that play "Yellow Bird," and coaster sets emblazoned with all the birds that John James Audubon managed to bend into a figure eight.

Standing upon my deerskin thunderbird rug, I cast my eye over an accumulation of wealth whose most prominent treasures included a throw crocheted by my sainted grandmother depicting a bird-draped Saint Francis of Assisi, a beer stein shaped into the likeness of a kori bustard, a turkey cleverly constructed out of porcelain vegetables, and a wood stove humidifier that looks like a muscovy and warbles like a canary.

Bear in mind that these are the keepers. The stuff we've relegated to the attic would make even the most tasteless Victorian pack rat long for the release of curbside pickup.

Of course, not all the bird-related stuff I get is useless or tasteless. But what's a person supposed to do with four copies of *Gone Birding?*

One Christmas (via my brother's secretary) I even received a gift copy of my book *The Feather Quest.* "Merry Christmas to my birdwatching brother," the inscription read. "I saw this book and thought of you."

I know that I'm not the only birder singled out for persecution. I have a naturalist writer friend named Diana whose friends also convey their affection with an avalanche of avian knickknacks. After the holidays we compare notes—a sort of birding bric-a-brac Big Day competition.

"So how many goldfinch/painted bunting/cardinal dish towels did you get this year?"

"Four."

"Beat you there. I got five. How about salt-and-pepper shakers with bluebirds feeding nestlings on them?"

"Two."

"Ooooh, tied score. What about lacquered pieces of driftwood boasting hand-painted kinglets?"

"If you let me count the goldcrest/firecrest combo along with the ruby-crowned and golden-crowned ensembles, three."

I used to think that the books that ended up on the bookstore bargain tables were publishing blunders—books whose sales simply could not realize an optimistic overprinting—but no longer. Now I believe that those half-priced coffee-table bird books are printed specifically to get people who know nothing about birds to buy them for friends who do.

And I've got an attic full of them.

"Oh, why," I pleaded to my hands, "can't I just once receive a normal present? A juicer. A breadmaker. Whatever happens to be in vogue this season. Why am I condemned to bear the brunt of so much misbegotten kindness?"

A single envelope remained on the table, one addressed in colored crayon, bearing the brand of a favorite niece. Bravely I opened the flap, withdrew a homemade birthday card, and stared at the lovingly drawn illustration. An illustration that replicated the outline of a child's hand. An illustration that resembled, not the expected bird, but—beyond all hope—a long-limbed, long-necked turtle.

"Oh blessed child," I whispered as tears flooded my eyes. "Favorite of my heart. You can count on a big fat check from Uncle Peter for the holidays."

Only then did I realize that "Happy Birthday" was written upside down. When righted, what had been a long-limbed turtle became just another turkey.

JUDGMENT DAY

The trail climbed where it should and dipped where it always has. That's one of the advantages of investing part of your youth in a 280-million-year-old ridge—long-term security in the futures market. Memory could not pinpoint the spot where I was supposed to leave the trail. But my feet knew the way. They veered and I followed. The place, when I came to it, was unmistakable.

In my mind I could see him standing there, that younger version of a much older man—the same man who was now surveying the spot where the avenue of a lifetime began. It was on this ridge, in the spring of 1976, that I stood for fifty-eight days—for 454 hours—counting the migrating hawks that passed. It was the project that gave me the skills and the standing that led to a career in the environmental field.

For 364 days a year, I have leave to look back and contemplate all that has transpired since that time—the privilege and perspective of age. But once each year, if I can, I go back to the ridge and let that person who was pass judgment on the person that is. I do it for perspective. I do it because a 280-million-year-old ridge offers a fixed point of reference to measure a life.

I wonder sometimes whether people whose lives are not anchored in the natural world have this advantage. I wonder, for instance, whether Bruce Springsteen ever goes back to the Asbury Park boardwalk. Whether the smell of cotton candy ignites memories. Whether the noise and crowds and flashing lights anchor perspective, offer haven, give counsel. I wonder whether in the noise and turmoil he can find himself honestly reflected and whether he likes what he sees.

I can see how this might be so. But boardwalks wear out and are replaced over time. Arcades trade hands, rides change theme music, people dress differently, talk differently. And boardwalks, unlike the natural world, are not neutral. They cater to the young. Would an aging rock star even want to go back to the boardwalk of his youth—particularly a rock star who now lives closer to the brighter lights of Vegas?

I looked at my old spot, at the boulders that had not moved in ten thousand years, at the view that remains unchanged—the perfect spot for a meeting of then and now.

I could see my younger self standing there. Wearing a sun-bleached 60/40 cloth jacket. Eyes hidden behind a pair of brand new Leitz 8×40 binoculars. Attention focused down-ridge as if nothing in the whole world mattered except finding that next bird of prey.

And do you know what? Nothing did.

"You're late," he said, not looking.

"You were always too early," I admonished, which was true. The kid was usually there before seven, even though hawks rarely went aloft before eight.

"You're a *year* late," he said. "You missed last year."

"Oh," I said, somewhat ruefully. "Couldn't get away."

The kid glanced my way, not even trying to hide his displeasure. Nothing, as far as he was concerned, was more important than hawk watching.

"New car," he noted, pointing to the parking area seven hundred feet below and a mile away.

"Same color as the Bug," I said, referring to the '72 Beetle the kid drove.

"Can you still pack all your worldly goods into it?" he demanded.

"No," I admitted, "I can't." The kid once asserted that he never wanted to own more things than he could stuff into a VW Bug and drive away with—a milestone he passed (and a promise he broke) in 1979.

"Getting kind of porky, aren't you," the kid challenged, with appalling candor and absolute accuracy. I was packing about ten more pounds than I was when we'd last met. Fact is, never again was I in the physical shape I was in when I first stood on this ridge.

"Can you still identify a hawk?" he challenged.

"Let's see," I said, picking up the gauntlet, filling my binoculars with sky.

The air over the Walnut Bluffs was wavy with heat—the heat that migrating hawks seek, to gain lift. A bird was turning circles just over the ridge—an accipiter. A mile away there were no field marks visible, and at this distance a bird's identity projects itself by hints and clues. The kid would someday write a book based on the secrets he was learning. But that milestone was still a decade away.

"Bird over the bluffs," I announced.

"Got it," he said. "Accipiter," he concluded.

"Cooper's hawk," I promised.

The bird left the bluffs and started for us. As distance diminished, subjectivity was stripped away and replaced by discernable features—a projecting head, a white-tipped tail, wing beats that were arthritically stiff—the things that make a Cooper's hawk a Cooper's hawk.

"Nice call," the kid admitted but grudgingly. Nobody likes to be beaten to a call at their own hawk watch.

"Thanks," I said. "Takes practice," I couldn't help adding. What I didn't tell him was that probability played a large part in the identification. Our vigil was being conducted at the peak of the Cooper's hawk migration. Sharp-shinned hawks, a near look-alike species, wouldn't be migrating in numbers until later.

The kid didn't know this—but then, when the kid was a kid, few people did.

"Well, at least you can still identify hawks," he admitted. "How's work?"

"Good," I pronounced, pleased that it was so. "But I'm pretty desk-bound. Not much time for birding."

"How much time?" the kid demanded.

"Just a few hours a week," I admitted.

The kid dropped his head in his hands and moaned—not that I blame him. Sometimes I do that myself. Then I thought of something that would please him.

"I turned down a job offer recently."

The kid brightened. "Doing what?" he wanted to know.

"Marketing director for an optics company."

"How come?" he asked.

"I like what I'm doing now."

"Another bird," he said, shutting down conversation. "Another . . . Cooper's hawk?" he asked more than said.

"Nice call," I judged.

There was silence for a time. Silence as we waited for birds to appear; silence as we waited for the hard questions to come.

"How's the writing?" The kid aspired to be a writer.

"Some of it's pretty good," I assessed. "But I think word processors are destroying any artistry in writing."

"What's a word processor?" he wanted to know.

"A machine that makes it easy to patch without fixing." I explained.

"How's the marriage?" he demanded.

"Infinitely better than the writing," I was pleased to say. "Worth your wait."

Morning became afternoon, and one by one the questions I carried to the ridge found their answers—on the neutral grounds of a timeless ridge. But the young inquisitor withheld judgment until one key question was addressed.

"What kind of music you listening to these days?"

"Some alternative rock," I said to uncomprehending eyes. "Some R.E.M. . . . a little Indigo Girls . . . Gin Blossoms, Enya . . ."

"Enya?" he demanded.

"Enya," I affirmed. "Kind of Celtic. Strains of Renaissance. You'd like her." Then I thought of something else he might like.

"Pink Floyd's got a new release."

"You still listen to Floyd?"

"Yeah," I admitted. "Sometimes."

There was no mistaking the approval in his eyes. "Awwwl right!" he said.

On my way down, I made a mental note to stop at the mall on the way home and pick up a couple of CDs. And a promise, if I could manage it, to try and lose some weight before next spring.

Part 2

STORIES

ABOUT

FRIENDS

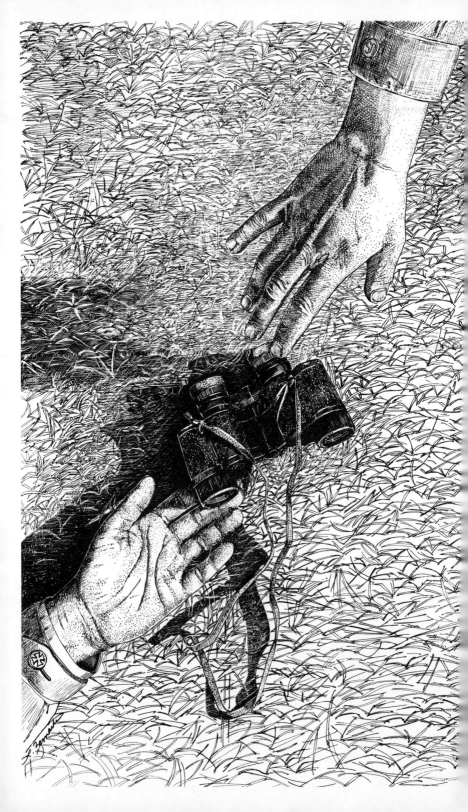

THE SOLDIER

This is a tribute to the Unknown German Soldier—the man who changed my life. I do not know his name. I do not know what part of Germany he came from. I do not even know if he was a birder or a naturalist—although he may have been. Most Germans, at least most of those it has been my privilege to meet, have an abiding love of nature.

The fact is I never met the Unknown German Soldier. I only know the man who met him, briefly, soldier to soldier. That man was my father, Corporal Dunne, an American GI in his early twenties who was playing a small part in a big war.

"I took them from a German who didn't need them anymore," was all my father said of the instrument I held in my hands—a pair of six-power binoculars. The device lived then in the drawer where all the tokens of my father's life were housed—chains attached to watches that didn't work, old coins that didn't shine, medals that proved my father was the hero every four-year-old knows his father to be.

But the thing I coveted most, the thing that I courted the risk of a spanking just to hold, was the magic look-through thing: the 'noculars. I had discovered that this sleek black instrument had the power to change the world.

If you looked through one end, it made the world smaller. But if you looked through the other end, the world got BIGGER and everything looked CLOSER.

The photos on the dresser . . . my mother in the kitchen . . . The birds! Feeding in the snow. Closer . . . and *alive*. They seemed, these sparrows and juncos and cardinals, more beautiful and more alive than anything in the whole wide world (whose limits lay just about where my parents' property line was).

Those magic 'noculars, taken from a soldier who didn't need them anymore, were the portals through which knowledge and discovery flowed, bird by bird. They were the catalyst that turned a suburban kid into a birder. They led me to a career as a New Jersey Audubon Society director and to the person I am today.

Fifty years after the war that brought the 'noculars into my hands, the instrument sits on my mantel, nestled amid the tokens of another man's life, my life. They are scarred by use and time, but they still function. I could take them out right now and filter birds through their prismed tubes, just as I did as a child—when the world was filled with undiscovered wonder and its borders were defined by my parents' property line.

Sometimes in the evening, when the fire draws down and my mind turns in upon itself, the 'noculars will catch my gaze the way they once drew my hands. Regarding them, I see once again the birds they brought to life and consider the strange fortune that brought them there.

At these times I find myself wondering about the Unknown German Soldier. Who he was. Whether he, like my father, had children. And if so, whether they have children now who are turning their eyes upon the world, seeking wonder.

Because if he did, and if they did, and if there was a way, I fancy that I would take those binoculars back to Germany and place them in their hands. To keep the magic flowing. To honor the man who was its source (though I do not know his name).

R.

The figure was standing beside the road, aware of my approach but not interested. He was looking off across a section of marsh, and he was looking for something specific. You could see this from a distance. You could see it from the body language projected by a birder on point.

The distance had narrowed to fifty feet before he turned his attention my way. I recognized him then, and the grin that creased his face showed that he recognized me. It was a sincere grin, but it did little to alter the balance of the face, which was a study in defeat.

"Oh hello, Pete," he said nodding, holding his heroic smile. "I figured I might see you around."

"Hello, R." I said, addressing him by name, grateful that I remembered it. "How's it going?"

"Oh," he said shyly, almost apologetically, "OK I guess."

And for a moment I let hope get the better of me. For a moment I thought that maybe R. and the world had come to better terms, but I was wrong.

"I'll be doing more birding now, 'cause I got laid off my job. I guess that's good news."

Of course, it wasn't good news, but as disclosures from R. went, it wasn't as bad as some. We'd met in 1979. R was seventeen and liked nature. I was ten years older and taught bird ID courses.

There was something tragic about R. even then, something that said his life would be stalked by hardship. But it had taken fifteen

years of compounded defeats to craft the image of passive sadness
I saw now. Fifteen years of plant closings, terminated apprentice-
ships, job layoffs, and a bout with alcoholism and its lasting con-
sequence: life without driving privileges in a mobile society.

"What do you have out there?" I asked, to get him off the subject of life's latest setback and to demonstrate my support by inviting his assistance. A person is never destitute so long as they have
something to share. And if that something is coveted by someone
else, you will always have standing in their eyes.

"I don't really know," he said, bringing his focus to bear on the
marsh again. "Some shorebird. I came out here to sort things out.
And these two birds jumped and squawked and flew. I wasn't familiar with the call. I'm waiting for them to come back."

"Snipe," I surmised but did not say. "How long you been
here?" I asked.

"Couple hours," he said. "Something to do," he explained, gesturing toward the marsh.

The explanation wasn't necessary, and it wasn't complete either.
Fact is, I understand how important something to do is when life
gets knocked off-balance. What R. left out of his explanation is
that things to do don't happen unless there are places to do them.
For me, for R., and for many other people, the places we turn to
when life takes a hard tack are the natural areas of our state.

Natural areas. Places with woodlands that close around you.
Places with ponds that can swallow a cannonade of tossed pebbles
and beaches that are open, unpeopled, and invite long walks.

I know what some people are thinking. "Diversion! That's all a
body needs when times get tough. Diversion, not nature." Work-
aholics can bury themselves in work. Physical fitness buffs go run
twenty miles. Gardeners plant a thousand bulbs or trim the rose
bushes or organize the shed. Nothing mystical about it.

And if natural history buffs want to go out in the woods and
peel the bark off of twigs in the name of therapy, well, what of it?

I don't think it's that simple, and I don't think a retreat into nature is that esoteric. I believe that *everyone* has an innate need to
interface with natural areas and that everyone responds to them. I

believe that nature heals better and faster than diversion and that people understand this *naturally.*

Consider Mr. M. He was a neighbor, an electrician and father to a flock of kids who were childhood chums of mine. His interest in nature, near as I could tell, was zero. And I never, ever, saw him enter the woods flanking our suburban development—except once.

It was the day after his son was killed in a traffic accident. I was off on one of my daily forays. We met on a pond side trail.

Of course, I was surprised to see him, and of course I couldn't find words to match his loss. Nobody can. But he understood my problem. He reached out an arm, touching me on the shoulder, thanking me without words. Then he walked on.

What was most remarkable about this meeting was not his kindness or his presence of mind. What was remarkable was his *state* of mind—if such things can be read in a face (and I believe they can). His face was the picture of serenity, of peace—the face of a person who had suffered greatly and won passage through grief.

I have seen this look depicted on the faces of statues in churches, and in such surroundings it is not out of place. In fact, it is beautiful. And once, on a woodland trail, I saw it on the face of the father of a childhood chum. It was not out of place there either.

There is something about the rhyme and pattern of nature that is eternal. There is something about weather and seasons and tides and lunar cycles that offers permanence and confidence.

A coworker, Pat Kane, offers summer programs for children, many of whom come from single-parent homes—many of whom are still caught in the turbulence left by a hard divorce. Pat uses nature as an antidote.

Says Pat: "Nature is something children can count on day after day. The leaves emerge in the spring. They drop to earth in the fall. They don't go on strike. They don't break promises. They just follow the natural cycle, and this is nature's way of saying that change is natural; change is OK."

Change is *natural.* It's only coming to grips with it that is hard.

I recall another person, a woman, who showed up at a hawk watch I was orchestrating many years ago. She was very quiet and very distant and this, in the right person, is very alluring.

It was several days before we spoke, several hours before I earned her confidence, and what I learned was that her father had just died. Rather than seek solace in people, she had opted to take her grief and her bearings beneath the river of birds migrating south. There she hoped to come to some accommodation with the change that had shaken her life.

Unlike my hawk-watching acquaintance, R. was as grateful for conversation as he was for the challenge presented by the birds he could not identify. My schedule was not pressing, so I indulged him. Listened to his account of the birds he had seen. Made encouraging noises in response to his plans to reap a harvest of new bird sightings this winter.

I did not disclose the identity of the mystery birds that bound him to the marsh. It would serve no purpose but to break the bond that had given momentary mooring to his life. Nor did I tell him that, unlike other shorebirds, snipe, once they have relocated, are not likely to return. What would be the point?

We parted eventually, wishing each other good luck. I left to complete the circuit of the trail I walk almost every day. And R.? R. stayed where he was. Just because there was nothing to see didn't mean that there was nothing to find—or that he hadn't already found it.

HAROLD

If you never met Harold Axtell—former whiz-kid at Cornell University's Laboratory of Ornithology, former trombone player on the Cunard Line, former curator of ornithology at the Buffalo Museum of Natural History (and my friend)—you missed a historic opportunity. Harold, until his death, resided in Fort Erie, Ontario. But this living link between the ornithologists of yesterday and the birdwatchers of today called New Jersey his home in October and November. When the winds turned cold and northerly, the path of birds turned south, and Harold's did likewise.

My introduction to this remarkable man occurred October 2, 1976, at Cape May Point. I was then a brash young hawk watcher with little skill and less standing. Harold was, according to rumor, a ghoulish perfectionist who could take every species of bird in North America down to its feather edges and who used questions the way the Spanish Inquisition used implements of torture.

I had been warned of Harold's imminent arrival. I had been told that the extraordinary numbers of Cooper's hawks I'd been reporting at Cape May Point had brought the Inquisitor's mind to bear on me.

This was 1976, remember, and that was an age that lived in the long shadow cast by the biocidal poison DDT—an age when Cooper's hawk numbers were reduced to a vestige. And Cooper's hawks were then, just as they are now, about as easy to distinguish from the very similar sharp-shinned hawk as Mercury automobiles are from Fords.

"Oh, *really,*" the impish-looking man fitting Harold's description said after I explained that I'd seen more than thirty Cooper's hawks the day before.

"My!" he exclaimed, studying my face. "Well!" he said, into the hand he'd raised to help support his chin. "I've been trying to learn how to tell Cooper's hawks from sharp-shinned hawks all of my life," said the man who knew more about hawk identification than Einstein knew about physics. "Would you mind very much if I stood next to you and studied every bird that you *believe* is a Cooper's hawk?"

I said no, but not because it was all right. I minded very much having the Inquisitor stand at my shoulder, second-guessing all my identifications. I said no because saying yes would have branded me a heretic, a liar, and someone *who couldn't tell a sharp-shinned from a Cooper's hawk* (surely the basest denunciation in all of hawk watching).

It was only seven in the morning, and the next two hours were the longest of my twenty-five-year-old life. Two thousand accipiters went past the hawk watch during that span, and *none* of them, as far as I could tell, bore the field marks of a Cooper's hawk.

I didn't know then, as everyone knows today, that sharp-shinneds are early risers and that Cooper's hawks like to feed before they fly, so during migration they are not commonly recorded in numbers until after nine. All I knew was that I was failing to back up my boastful record with evidence and that the Inquisitor's skepticism was growing.

Finally, around nine, a bird appeared that seemed to have a head larger than a sharp-shinned hawk's; a tail that was round, not square-tipped; and pale underparts that gave the face the appearance of being covered by a hangman's hood.

"How about that one?" I said, putting my own head squarely in the Inquisitor's noose.

Harold focused his binoculars on the bird and studied it in silence. Seconds mounted and still the Inquisitor held his judgment in check.

"Yessss," he said finally, and the word put a smile on his face that stayed. "That one seems to me to be a Cooper's hawk also."

I tallied nearly a hundred Cooper's hawks that day. And Harold? Harold saw nearly a hundred also.

Harold, of course, was not a ghoul—in fact, anything but. He was, very simply, a gentle man, driven by an exquisitely inquisitive mind, who loved truth and nature and found no need to distinguish between the two. He was *not* a ghoul—but as a man in his seventies, his features had taken a somewhat gnomish tack.

Harold's face sagged like a discarded mattress and was as wrinkled as an unmade bed. His clothing was equally weathered but eminently utilitarian. His workaday uniform consisted of iron gray trousers, a gray-green work shirt, and a fedora so shopworn that even the wind didn't want it. In the cherished image of the eccentric birdwatcher, Harold *always* wore rubber galoshes. Always.

There was almost always the hint of a smile tugging at the corners of Harold's mouth—as if he and the Creator were privy to some private joke beyond the grasp of mere mortals. But when conversation turned to the subject of birds, the mouth turned serious and the eyes followed suit.

It is no small understatement to say that Harold was a talker. He could pursue a subject for hours and chase digressions down trails that branched and branched. But no matter how many digressive paths Harold might investigate, he never failed to backtrack with skill and follow the mother subject to a conclusion.

Once during a lull in the migration, I asked Dr. Axtell how he became interested in birds. The reply consumed all of one day and most of the next.

You must understand that when a person asked a question of Harold, he felt honor-bound and duty-bound to offer as complete a response as possible. Harold loved truth—the whole truth—and I think he never quite understood how or why most people are content with less.

I recall a day, and never without pain, when Harold met a birding group led by someone he knew. Someone made the mistake of posing a question to Harold, a depthful one, one that demanded an answer that went on for more time than errant birders, visiting a birding hotspot at peak season, are accustomed to give.

First one member of the group grew antsy and slipped away . . . then another . . . and another until all were gone. Harold, who was concentrating on the answer and his feet, never noticed until he looked up and found himself alone.

I was over a hundred feet away, but the look of dismay that creased his well-creased face was unmistakable and it drove right to the heart. He seemed about to cry. Then he seemed about to leave. But he did neither. Instead he bowed his head once more, and he continued speaking until the full truth was spoken.

Even though no one except God and Harold wanted to hear it.

It was at once one of the saddest and greatest things I have ever witnessed. And I would give much, *much,* to know the substance of a truth so profound that it could master such hurt.

In late November, when migration nears its end, the air holds the morning chill. The sun rises late, and the hawks rise later. You can see all that there is to see of a flight by arriving at ten.

The birds spiral high. They gather in sunlight-colored clusters that shine against the sky. If the winds hold true (and you pray that the winds hold true), the flight may last till noon. That is when conversation on the hawk watch platform fills the void left by the departed birds. That is when Harold is most missed.

I have never told anyone this, and I hesitate to tell it now, fearing maybe that it will not be believed. But in November, the air that holds the chill also holds a sound. Sometimes it is like the murmur of distant geese. Sometimes it sounds like an orchestra playing a lively dance tune behind doors that are closed and locked.

But sometimes it sounds like the scuff of rubber-shod feet, falling on a gravel parking lot, that draw no closer and only fade until the sound exists only in memory.

COLVILLE DIARY

Day 1—We didn't wait for the plane to disappear before starting to portage our gear down to the river. The denizens of this un-named (and probably unmapped) tundra pond—oldsquaw, glau-cous gulls, greater scaup, and red-throated loons—didn't waste time getting back to the business of nesting, either. In summer, days may be endless on Alaska's North Slope, but seasons are short.

"Looks like we beat the mosquitoes," I said to Bob Dit-trick, friend, companion, and cofounder of Wilderness Birding Adventures.

"Looks like the weather god isn't going to hammer us today either," he added, grinning.

Yes, we were pretty lucky—privileged, actually. Here we were in one of the planet's last great wildernesses, poised for a nine-day trip down the Colville, one of the grandest rivers in the Arctic. We had no schedule, no obligations, and no greater ambition than to savor everything.

"Arctic warbler," Bob said, nodding toward a nearby willow thicket.

"Got it," I said, completing the litany, training my binoculars on the only life bird the trip was likely to produce. "Nice," I said when my appraisal was over. "Now I can enjoy myself."

Day 2—We rose late, eight or so in the morning, and left later. Gray-cheeked thrushes were *everywhere*. I mean, EH-VREE-WHERE (almost as common as Arctic warblers). I decided to test the conventional wisdom that once you see a life bird they become dirt-common. I decided to test it by keeping a running tab of the Arctic warblers encountered on the trip.

Breakfast was cold cereal and French-roast coffee. We shared it with bluethroats, yellow wagtails, and four species of sparrow, all the while enjoying a duet offered by winnowing snipe and yodeling oldsquaws. Hunting rough-legs were a visual blight.

It took no more than an hour to put our canoe together, a folding fabric affair of Norwegian make and design. Fully loaded it rode like a grebe.

Our put-in point was the Ipnavik, a merry little stream that writhes like an eel and nips at riverside bluffs. The bluffs are the key. They host the nesting raptors that make the Colville and its tributaries one of the greatest raptor factories in the world.

As a graduate student, ornithologist Tom Cade had navigated the Colville and mapped the bluffs. We served up lunch at one of his single-digit sites, within easy scoping distance of a pair of tundra peregrines. Dinner—spaghetti, garlic bread, and salad with vinaigrette dressing—was prepared at the site that served up a white gyrfalcon.

"Only the second white one I've seen here," said Bob.

"Pass the sauce, please," I replied.

"I figured we did thirty-one miles today," Bob estimated.

"Good job on the dressing," I agreed. "Any bread left?"

Day 3—You will want to know the dates of our trip. There are no dates. You may want to know what time we rose. There was no time. There was nothing but the day, which was at once as long and as short as an Arctic summer. If the questions had been raised earlier in this accounting, I might have had an answer. But by Day 3, I had put the outside world behind. This was the day I took my wallet out of my pocket and put it in the bottom of my duffel bag, and my watch went with it.

We got up when we got up. We left when the last of the coffee was gone. The rhythm of the day was set by the stroke of paddles, the hiss of sand in the river, and the electric *zinging* of riverside redpolls.

Intervals were marked by lunch (hummus, cheese, and rye crisps) and dinner (chile and red wine). We found three peregrine nests, ten nesting rough-legs . . . and added ten more Arctic warblers to the *fifty-one!* tallied the day before.

Yes, it's true. Empirical evidence supports the premise that once you see a life bird, they become dirt-common.

Day 4—Still no mosquitoes and still no retribution from the weather god. The lenticular clouds that appeared last evening were probably a ruse.

It's warm too—fifty to sixty degrees, and the heat building in our tent is the prod that drives us out in the morning. There's little reason to hurry. Birds are everywhere, and our campsites are chosen to be within easy sight of any peregrine nest worth viewing. Today's birds are on a bluff across from a gravel bar the size of Key West.

After a cheese omelet, hash browns, and coffee, we climbed a nearby cliff and took stock of the world from the eroded saddle of the ridge—between the severed ends of a petrified log. We ate a candy bar, picked through assorted fossils, savored a grizzly bear and her two cubs, and watched while the male peregrine harassed the recticies off the neighboring rough-legged hawk.

Twenty-three miles (and twenty-three Arctic warblers) later, we parked for the night on a sandbar that was a mosaic of wolf tracks and (you guessed it) across from a peregrine nest.

"What's for dinner," I inquired.

"Jambalaya," Bob said, enunciating with relish. "Cheesecake for dessert. The weather god," he added, "loves cheesecake."

Day 5—Woke to fog in the distance and the whine of a mosquito in camp.

Uh oh.

"That fog is associated with eight degrees centigrade," Bob confided. We don't want to see too much of that!" Of course, we

had a more immediate problem—an impending insect problem—
so we went off to check the status of the hatch. The tundra pools
were a wiggling mass of mosquito larvae, but at least they were
still larvae.

There were pancakes and golden eagles for breakfast—first
time for both on the trip. The eagle, a subadult, was intent on
catching one of the local flock of white-fronted geese. A territorial
rough-legged hawk finally drove the eagle out of the area.

We put twenty-two hard miles on the canoe, into head winds
most of the way. Then, rushing to put up the tent before a shower
caught us, I snapped a pole.

"What about just sleeping out?" I asked.

"That," said the co-owner of Wilderness Birding Adventures as
he calmly repaired the pole, "is like dropping your drawers to the
weather god with your hands manacled."

Day 6—It rained overnight and we woke to the sound of . . . *a
mosquito in the tent!!!*

"GET IT!" Bob commanded.

I made a one-handed grab and missed.

"It's real bad luck to let the first one get away," Bob said.
"That's our last night with the door open."

I'm not going to tell you that Bob is a superstitious man. I'm just
going to tell you that he is a very successful guide who leads birding groups all over the Arctic while offering a level of comfort that
clients find easy to accept but hard to believe. Far be it from me to
question the foundation of his success.

It became abundantly clear that we were falling out of favor
with the weather god as well as the Keeper of the Hatch. A squad-
ron of thunderheads stalked us all day, and we had to play cat and
mouse with one particularly tenacious cloud (probably their cap-
tain). We finally gave our shadow the slip by hiding out in an old
river channel. That's where Bob spotted the cave with the pyramid
of whitewash projecting from the floor—a pyramid surrounded by
a two-foot pile of reincarnated ptarmigan who had come back to
earth in the form of gyrfalcon pellets.

That evening we set up camp on a gravel bar across from . . . Well, you guess.

Day 7—Zero miles by canoe. After a bear mush breakfast, we decided to hike up the Oolamnavigovik River, a Colville tributary. The status of the river and surrounding sixty-three *million* acres, currently under the jurisdiction of the Bureau of Land Management, is under dispute. Bob was due to testify on behalf of wilderness designation, and he wanted fresh observations.

The first part of the hike cut through willow thickets boasting bushes fifteen feet high *and* a trio of gray jays, a bird whose established range (according to published range maps) stops south of the North Slope. Not at all unexpected but just as interesting, we stumbled upon a redpoll nest with five brown-spotted blue eggs. Gorgeous!

Atop a bluff that looked like a slag heap worked over with a blowtorch, we dined on reindeer sausage, cheese, and pilot bread and watched grizzly bears and caribou moving across the tundra. The wind was cool, the sun was warm. We stretched out like lizards, watching the sun through molten eyelids until the clouds came up and the world got colder.

Day 8—The world got real cold. And wet! The weather god was closing in, but he'd made a strategic error. He'd waited until we were in our tent.

Our arrangement with the pilot was for him to come look for us, so, not having a rendezvous site, we weren't in any hurry to get wet. Instead, we enjoyed some downtime in the tent—reading, sleeping, writing (sleeping), watching the local raven kids cutting up and the peregrine couple arguing over mealtimes.

About midafternoon the female peregrine set up a ruckus, which turned out to be directed at a dark brown critter the size and shape of a coffee table.

"Wolverine!" Bob shouted.

We watched from the tent as the Arctic weasel tried to avoid the peregrine's efforts to cut it down to the dimensions of a footstool.

It was clear that the wolverine wanted the eggs—but maybe not at the asking price, the price of getting flayed. The dispute was finally settled by outside arbitration. A Canada goose nesting below the peregrine's ledge flushed, exposing her clutch of eggs (and offering the wolverine an alternative it could live with).

"How 'bout breakfast . . . or dinner?" Bob invited.

I moved for dinner. Spaghetti, mushroom sauce, and the last of the wine. A fine way to celebrate life mammals—and the longest night of the year. Even the rain stopped.

After dinner we loaded up and traveled four miles downriver— away from the peregrine nest and astride a stretch of river that would take the plane easily. Around midnight a sucker hole opened in the overcast, giving us a glimpse of the midnight sun on the longest day of the year. From the thicket, an Arctic warbler broke into song—number 185.

Not a bad day.

Day 9—We couldn't sleep in, not on pickup day. Bush pilots keep loose hours, but when they arrive is when you're supposed to be ready. It wasn't even noon when Bob said, "I hear a plane." Then I heard it too. A distant hum that sounded like dread.

The sky was clearing. Sunlight was playing across rain-spattered hills and reaching for the river.

"Looks like it's going to be a nice day," I observed.

"Does," Bob agreed, sadly.

During our nine days in the Arctic, we had heard several planes but none that had intruded upon us. This one was different. And though there are many ugly sounds in the world, one of the worst is the sound of the bush plane that is coming to pick you up. In fact, I can only think of one sound worse. That is sound of the weather god laughing.

THE LAST BIG DAY

The robins were starting their evening song as our van turned off the macadam and onto the rutted lane. It had been fourteen hours since we'd first navigated this nameless pine barrens tract. The robins had been singing then too.

Branches raked the side of the vehicle, and puddles leaped for the safety of the underbrush. Our van bucked, and occupants had to use both hands to keep their seats bonded to the seats.

At the end of the lane, sandwiched between a field and a pig farm, we stopped. Almost immediately a large, soot-colored bird lofted out of the pen and into view. A burst of adrenaline cut through our fatigue, opening channels to the deductive centers of our brains—but to little avail and no gain.

"Turkey vulture," several voices intoned flatly. We'd already seen turkey vulture during the day. And on the World Series of Birding, every species found counts just once.

Another vulture joined the first, another TV. Then another, and another. It looked as though things were moving toward a repeat of our earlier, failed effort.

Just as disappointment was beginning to seem certain, another bird fled the pen. Its body jerked, its wings pumped, and white-tipped flight feathers flashed.

"It's a black [vulture]," someone shouted (and it might have been me).

"Got it," said Pete Bacinski.

"Got it," said Linda, my wife.

"Got it," said Rick Radis.

Bruce Cavey, our World Series of Birding team sponsor from Zeiss Optical (and a neutral observer), remained neutral.

All eyes turned toward the last member of our World Series team, a man whose face is as familiar to birdwatchers as Washington's profile on a one dollar bill—the man who in 1934 crafted a book that turned a scientific study into a populist pursuit enjoyed by millions.

Did he get on the bird before it disappeared? Could we count it as a unanimous sighting on our World Series list?

"Yes," he said, nodding. "Black vulture for sure," said Roger Tory Peterson, the dean of North American birding. It was the 160th species we'd tallied during our long day of birding, and it would be the last bird.

May 15, 1993, was not the first opportunity I'd had to bird with Dr. Peterson, who at eighty-four was the oldest participant in that year's World Series of Birding, an annual contest sponsored by the New Jersey Audubon Society. The author of *Field Guide to the Birds* was also a member of my team on the very first World Series of Birding, held in 1984.

I was thirty-two then, the director of the Cape May Bird Observatory and the instigator of an idea for a competitive event that would raise money for the environment based upon the number of birds seen. He was seventy-four and a legend.

It would have been unthinkable to contemplate a birdwatching competition and not consult the wisdom of birding's grand master. So one day, early in the planning process, I telephoned Dr. Peterson at his home in Connecticut to state my case and learn his mind.

Would he favor the idea? Would he give it his blessing? I needn't have worried.

"Whose team can I be on?" asked the man who pretty nearly invented birding. "Can I be on yours? We should start at Troy Meadows at midnight, don't you think? Then move on to the hills above Boonton for migrants at dawn. . . ."

In case you are not a birder, this is the birding equivalent of being invited to play a round of golf with Lee Trevino, jam with Eric

Clapton, or shoot hoops with Magic Johnson. It's like calling the Vatican for directions and having the pope ask whether he can go to church with you on Sunday.

And on May 19, 1984, Roger Tory Peterson marshaled the efforts of the Guerrilla Birding Team (as we called ourselves), carried us to a total of 201 species, and swept us to victory in the first annual World Series of Birding.

I recall well our dawn site on that morning of the contest. We stood on the old elevated railroad bed near Waterloo, New Jersey, sifting the sounds of a dawn chorus through our ears, filtering out and identifying each newly wakened songster.

I recall how Roger Peterson stood: with his feet spaced, his ear turned, and his white-frocked head inclined toward the woodlands and fields beyond.

Every bird adding its song to the chorus was identified by Dr. Peterson almost as soon as the notes left its beak. He punctuated each bird's identity—eastern phoebe, golden-winged warbler, northern waterthrush—with an index finger jabbed at the sky.

It was a glorious dawn and a wonderful day, and it set the pace for the World Series that followed. And the event grew—grew in measure with its success. Where thirteen teams took to the field in 1984, now there are more than fifty. Where once less than fifty hard-core birders participated, now hundreds take to the field.

But during a decade of growth, that first World Series maintained one singular distinction. It marked the only time that Roger Tory Peterson was a participant. This shortfall was remedied on May 15, 1993, when Dr. Peterson returned.

Ten years is a long time in the measure of human lives. Infants become spelling bee champions. Spelling bee champions grow up and become graduate students or fighter pilots or perhaps parents with future spelling champions of their own.

Older men with a lifetime of achievements already behind them get older, and it was an older Roger Tory Peterson who came to Cape May for the 1993 World Series of Birding.

The years, he was frank to admit, had fallen between his ears and the world somewhat. Many warbler songs had become discordant, and blackpoll warblers, whose ethereal notes barely brush the human registry, had grown disquietingly quiet in his backyard in Connecticut.

His eyes, too, were a concern to him. Two cataract operations had greatly improved his vision, but they could not give back the visual acuity of the twenty-five-year-old artist who published the field guide to the birds.

In 1984 we ran a World Series route that covered much of the state, but in 1993 our ambitions were more tempered. We elected to cover Cape May County alone. It would give us more time to bird and take hours off the day at both ends.

Frustration was our companion from the start. There was a screech owl that would not call, great-horned owls that refused our invitation to engage in a duet, and that clutch of black vultures already mentioned that missed their dawn appointment.

Fog prevented us from catching the morning flight of seabirds off Cape May Point, and a night without migrating birds left branches bare. Our list suffered accordingly.

But there were successes too. Like the maddeningly intermittent Louisiana waterthrush that sang a lusty greeting on the morning when it counted. Like the pomarine jaeger that sprang full-blown from the surf and the red-shouldered hawk whose screams reached Roger's ears first—having eluded all of ours.

And at the Sunday awards brunch, when the team captains rose to offer an accounting of themselves and their team's fortune, it was Roger Peterson who brought the room to silence with his recollections of Big Day birding in days gone by and of the Cape May he knew sixty years ago. Then the lines formed—the lines of autograph seekers that follow Dr. Peterson everywhere. People whose lives had been touched by the man in front of them and who wanted to affirm his gift with their thanks.

Despite his tiredness, despite the admonishing eye of wife Ginny, he accommodated them all, affixing his signature to the books and the World Series bulletins passed his way—the bulletins listing the names of those teams and those individuals who shared in Roger Tory Peterson's last Big Day.

Part 3

STORIES

ABOUT

BIRDS . . .

IN PRAISE OF JAYS

When I think of August, the first thing I recall is silence. The resident birds who greeted each morning with song in June and July are indifferent now, their need to sing rings around their breeding territories gone with the season. The passage birds too are reticent. A "chip" is all you'll get.

So it's silence (not the heat, not the baked earth smell) that I think of first when I recall August woodlands. But the second thing I recall is the sound of a band—a roving, brassy-voiced band of blue jays that move through the summer-tired trees like a crested wave.

They surround you. Taunt you. Jeer at you. Accuse you of trespass, premeditated passage, upright locomotion, and indifference to blue jays. They lean into your face like drill sergeants chewing out a bumbling recruit, screaming blue murder. Then turning on their branches, looking toward the forest for support, the harangue stops as quickly as it started.

The troop murmurs among itself for a time. Members scratch a few feather lice. Pick at a leaf or two. Sidestep down a branch and regard you slyly. "Just a joke," they seem to be saying. "Nothing personal." Then the troop flies off, seeking devilment and diversion elsewhere.

As they leave, I find it hard not to smile and thank both heaven and earth for blue jays.

There are eleven jay species in North America: blue, Steller's, gray-breasted, Florida scrub, western scrub, island scrub, pinion, gray, green, brown, and Clark's nutcracker. All are bold. All are brash. Most are flamboyantly garbed, and—with the exception of the gray jay of northern forests—the males, females, and young of the species are virtually identical. Only one is found in my home state of New Jersey, or has ever been found in New Jersey! *Cyanocitta cristata*—the "noisy coxcomb," in the words of Washington Irving; "beauty covering a multitude of sins," in the estimate of Neltje Blanchan, a turn-of-the-century bird lover.

"He is mischievous as a small boy, destructive as a monkey, deft at hiding as a squirrel," Blanchan goes on to say about the bird in her famous treatise *Bird Neighbors*. "He is unsociable and unamiable, disliking the society of other birds. His harsh screams, shrieks, and most aggressive and unmusical calls seem often intended maliciously to drown the songs of the sweet-voiced singers."

Me? I see another side to this strikingly plumaged, year-round resident of forests, parks, and suburban haunts. I see a flamboyant fraud, a cherub in truant's clothing.

I have had opportunity to hold blue jays in the hand—several nestlings and a larger number of adults that I had netted and subsequently banded. Bold-as-brass reputation notwithstanding, hold a blue jay in a hand and they become docile as lambs. They don't struggle like chickadees. They don't shriek like a starling. They just lie there, eyes glazed, bills agape, breath shallow. The brass doesn't show again until the bird is released.

During the nesting season too, the birds are reticent, furtive. One summer a pair of blue jays nested in a spruce in our backyard. The loose-stick nest with the woven rootlet core was placed deep in the branches and two-thirds of the way up the fifteen-foot tree.

The male never flew directly to the tree while Linda and I watched. He would sit in a cross-yard mulberry and wait until certain we weren't turned his way; then, launching himself, he'd fly silently to the bottommost branches of the spruce. After a moment's pause, he'd move up the tree, branch by branch, until the nest was gained. Then, his morsel offered and accepted, he'd leave—always by the back door.

The docile nature of blue jays has its limits (as many a neighborhood cat has learned). If not for its crest and striking plumage, the bird would be famous for its bill. Large and formidable, it serves as both weapon and tool, as well suited for poking holes in too inquisitive noses as into white oak acorns.

But nothing seems to earn the ire of blue jays more than the sight of a roosting owl. On scores of occasions I have been led to the location of roosting owls by orienting toward the screamed alarm calls of jays. They surround the bird, leaning perilously close, screaming insults and stooping toward the unfortunate owl's head. But why?

Some animal behaviorists say the motive is altruism. By mobbing the owl, scientists explain, the jays are warning other jays (and other forest birds) that a danger lies close at hand. Watch out! Mobbing may also serve to drive a predator away, thus removing the threat.

Me? I think it's just showing off. The way I translate "Jay, jay, jay," is "Nah, nah, nah." When I see blue jays taunting owls, it reminds me of a troop of youngsters taunting the playground bully. "Look at me. Look at me," the birds seem to be sassing. "See how close I can get. Betcha I'm braver than you are."

I've watched blue jays edge toward perched Cooper's hawks, stalk to within several feet of their mortal enemy. When the hawk charges, the jays retreat, scolding and screaming. It's like a game of tag, albeit a high-stakes game (as the number of feather blue fairy rings scattered about the forest floor attests).

I'm also convinced that the memory of blue jays is acute. On a number of occasions, I have followed the sound of scolding jays to a predator roost site where I have seen owls and jays interacting before, only to discover that the jays are engaged in pantomime. The birds are screaming—sometimes poking their heads into an empty cavity, sometimes hovering around an owlish-looking perch. But there is no predator, at least not in the present.

Does the location act as a visual stimulus, triggering a mobbing reaction? Or said another way, is it possible that the jays are *acting out* an old campaign for their amusement? I realize that the difference between acting in play and reenacting is no modest cerebral leap. But if any bird is capable of weaving legend and pageantry into its life, it's the "noisy coxcomb."

Even if the bird is not a mime, it is certainly a mimic, and a good one at that. I have heard blue jays imitate the calls of red-shouldered hawks with such accuracy that whole Big Day birding teams have fallen for the ruse. The birds offer a fair rendering of the calls of Cooper's hawks and red-tailed hawks too.

Though a year-round resident in my northern state, blue jays are migratory. In late September and early October, groups of birds can be seen moving along ridge tops. In Cape May, in October and in May, there are mornings when hundreds and perhaps thousands of jays can be seen.

They fly in loose globular flocks that occupy a horizontal plane. They flap more or less constantly and look toward the open water of Delaware Bay with no small amount of trepidation—and with good reason. Jays after all are forest birds. If danger threatens and the birds are out over the open bay, they have no place to hide, which they try and do whenever danger threatens.

Suddenly one of the troop calls the alarm—a single, strangled "Jay." As one the whole airborne troop executes a crash dive, plummeting straight down into the trees, a hundred (or two or three hundred) feathered darts in accelerated free-fall.

If the problem is a hawk, the birds wait until it goes by, then launch themselves from the trees and continue on. If the escape was triggered by a false alarm (i.e., if one of the members of the troop pulled the communal rip cord without sufficient provocation), it seems that the heads poking out of the foliage have an accusatory demeanor. It's as if each is accusing the other of being the whistle-blower.

Blue jays have their bad points to balance the good. Yes, they sometimes prey on the nestlings of other birds. Yes, they are aggressive at feeders and hog all the sunflower seed.

But when the days turn cold and all the brightly colored birds of summer have abandoned us, it's the jays who add color to the landscape. And when the summer heat steals the song from the mouths of birds, woodlands still ring with the cries of blue jays.

SMALL-HEADED FLYCATCHER.

SEEN YESTERDAY.

HE DIDN'T LEAVE HIS NAME.

I'm not asking you to believe the story you are about to read, not willing to compromise the bond of trust that binds one birder to another. Frankly, I'm not sure I believe it myself.

It's a story whose roots are buried in the origins of birding and whose branches rake the future. A story of discovery and wonder and achievement. A story of pride and selfishness and loss.

It's a birding story, and it began—as you will come to learn—nearly two centuries ago. But my small part began on a typical, lackluster morning in June—the time of year just after the last of the mourning warblers straggle through and before the lesser yellowlegs fly.

It was Monday, a workday. I ambled up the Cape May Bird Observatory steps, the sound of laughing gulls in my ears. I walked in, made coffee, wandered over to my office, and started leafing through several days' accumulation of Post-It notes, crumpling them as I read.

There were half a dozen reminders from a snarling pack of editors, advising that assorted drop-dead deadlines had passed. There were three messages from my mother and two from my boss, Tom Gilmore—all bound by a thematic thread that might be summarized "It would certainly be nice to hear from you again someday. Call."

One message was from Berny's Auto Repair Shop. Berny is the guy who keeps *Hawks in Flight* coauthor Clay Sutton's aging Toyota and my vintage Saab in repair. This is the same guy who bought a yacht and named it *Hawks in Flight* in our honor. That message read: "Sorry, Pete. It's not just the linkage." Kathy, my administrative coordinator, had drawn one of those insipid smile faces next to this one.

At the bottom of the mound was one final message—a cryptic one that made no sense. It read: "Pete: Small-headed flycatcher. Seen yesterday. He didn't leave his name."

Small-headed flycatcher! Small-headed flycatcher? You know, there is nothing like working in the old natural history racket for fielding crank calls. You name 'em, we get 'em. You can mark your calendar by them.

In March the phone lines are jammed with calls about the old kamikaze cardinals throwing themselves against the window. In April it's woodpeckers banging on drainpipes (and what are we going to do about it). May and June—the dreaded BBCs (the baby bird calls) start pouring in. And come July and August, the phone lines are flooded with SOS appeals for laughing gulls with busted wings.

You know, if there was one laughing gull left on earth and I was living in a cave in Tibet, the thing would fly into a telephone line and bust a wing, and someone would bring it to me.

And *then* it's October and . . .

Ring . . . ring . . . ring . . . "Good morning. Cape May Bird Observatory."

"Oh, I'm so glad you are there. Oh, I hope you can help me. We have this bird. And it is all brown with black spots, and it has a red spot on the back of its head and a great big black V on its chest. It's been sitting on our lawn all morning and . . ."

One day I even tried answering the phone with the greeting "It's a flicker," but it didn't make any difference. Callers still insisted on describing the bird.

But as for small-headed flycatchers . . . Well, *that* was one for the record book.

The name meant nothing to me. The message demanded no further action. The Post-It note joined the others in the wastebasket, and *that* would have been *that* except . . .

Except one week later a manila envelope arrived in the mail containing a colored pencil drawing and a handwritten letter.

The words were learned, florid—the product of a scholarly mind. The handwriting was bent, corrupted—the product of an aged, palsied hand. The letter described a bird of approximately five inches in length and what the writer judged to be "eight inches in extent."

I figured that meant wingspan.

"The upper parts," as he described them, "were dull yellow-olive; the wings dusky brown, edged with lighter; the greater and lesser coverts tipped with white; the low parts dirty white, stained with dull yellow, particularly on the upper parts of the breast; the tail dusky brown and two exterior feathers marked like those of many with a spot of white on the inner vanes; head remarkably small; bill broad at the base, furnished with bristles, and notched near the tip; legs dark brown; feet yellowish; eye dark hazel."

The drawing, though painfully done, replicated the description. It resembled a Nashville warbler with wing bars or maybe an immature yellow warbler with an outsized eye. Both the letter and the drawing were signed "John Hancock." The address: Greenwich (pronounced "green witch"), New Jersey.

Now I know most of the birders in New Jersey and I didn't know John Hancock—never heard of the man. But I did know Greenwich, a beautiful old shipping town astride the Cohansey River, a watercourse known in history books as the site of a "tea party" in league *with,* but less celebrated *than* the famous tax revolt in Boston Harbor. I returned to the letter and the drawing.

He said that the flycatcher lived in an "alba" cedar swamp not far from his home. He said the bird had *not* been there before. Not since his youth. And possibly, *possibly* not since "AMERICAN ORNITHOLOGY."

AMERICAN ORNITHOLOGY, underlined, all caps. I liked that part. Was this fellow Hancock trying to tell me that he'd discovered a new North American species or what? "A juvenile yellow warbler," I concluded, studying the drawing, considering the several discordant points but dismissing them. Swamp woodlands aren't exactly prime habitat for yellow warblers. And a fledgling yellow warbler in mid-June in New Jersey is about two weeks too early. But that's what the drawing depicted, and what else could it be?

Pine warbler? Uh-uh. Wing bars weren't prominent enough. Nashville warbler? Not nesting in South Jersey, no way. Philadelphia vireo? Even *less* likely—though still a heck of a lot more plausible than the scenario that this fellow Hancock was dishing up.

I drafted a quick reply, offered my opinion, *then* realized that there was no return mailing address. So I put the letters, mine and his, and the drawing back in the manila envelope. And set it in the top compartment of my work tray until I could deal with it. It was still there when I left Cape May Bird Observatory two months later to take another post, with New Jersey Audubon. And that was nine years ago . . .

But even so. Even *now* I can still see it sitting there. The most important ornithological document I've ever set hands on. And I have ransacked CMBO's files. Torn closets apart. Gutted a landfill's worth of bundled documents, searching for that envelope. But it's gone, lost. And it would have been lost beyond recall too, except . . .

Except that, several years ago, Linda gave me a present. Four framed lithographs drawn by famed bird artist Alexander Wilson. "For the new dining room," she explained. "Happy birthday."

Two were dominated by raptors. Another depicted marsh birds. The last, sparrows. Tucked in the upper-right-hand corner of the plate featuring the great horned owl. Sandwiched between hawk owl and barn owl was . . .

A small yellow bird.

A bird that shed any names experience could bring to bear.

A bird that I could not identify—but a bird I *knew* I had seen depicted somewhere before.

At the bottom of the plate, written in Wilson's frail script, was a name. That name.

Now, I'm not going to say I believed it. Believed that some old gomer from Backwash, New Jersey, had rediscovered a bird that is substantiated by *no* modern records. Is not backed up by a specimen in any collection. And whose very existence is clouded by controversy, denial, and doubt. Both Wilson and Audubon *claimed* to have discovered the species. The bird was then—and it remains today—the very epitome of the rivalry (yes, even enmity) that existed between these twin pillars of American ornithology.

It was Wilson who beat Audubon to press, who offered his account of the bird he claimed to have collected along the banks of the Schuylkill River in 1810 (maybe 1811—the account is unclear).

"It was remarkably active," Wilson says in his description, "running, climbing, and darting about among the opening buds and blossoms with extraordinary agility. From what quarter of the United States or of North America it is a wanderer, I am unable to determine, having never met with an individual of the species."

Wilson subsequently determined that the bird nested in the swamps of South Jersey. He collected, he said, "several individuals there, in June." *Muscicapa minuta,* he named the bird, a privilege accorded the discoverer of a new species.

"Not so," said Audubon, and, when his *Birds of America* was published a quarter-century later, he said a good deal more. "When Alexander Wilson visited me at Louisville," said John James Audubon, "he found in my already large collection of drawings, a figure of the present species, which, being at that time unknown to him, he copied, and afterwards published in his great work, but without acknowledging the privilege that had thus been granted him. I have more than once regretted this, not by any means so much on my own account, as for the sake of one to whom we are so deeply indebted for his elucidation of our ornithology."

This is how a gentleman called another gentleman a liar and a thief in those days.

No, I'm not going to say I actually believed this improbable scenario. That as I lay awake that night, staring at the ceiling, I gave it more than the ghost of a chance—thought of it as anything more than a story line worth pursuing.

I'm not going to tell you that the next morning when I walked into Arnold's General Store in Greenwich, inquired about John Hancock, and learned that at the age of eighty-seven he had died, that I was much more than *disappointed.*

Or that when I stood on the porch of the old brick house. Where six generations of Hancocks have lived and died. And talked my way past the brittle smile of the widow Hancock. That I thought this visit would actually come to, *lead to . . .*

Something that no one reading these words should ever believe.

Not when I entered the book-lined library. Not when I saw the pressed and labeled sedges . . . and mounted butterflies . . . and Indian artifacts . . . and stuffed birds . . . and original Audubon lithographs . . .

Not when I saw. In a glass-fronted bookcase. The ancient corner-thumbed copies of *American Ornithology.*

Not when I inquired. "About a *bird.*" That her husband discovered a few years ago. "In a swamp." And did he ever mention it?

And received a curt, Quakerish nod.

Not even when I asked whether she knew where the swamp was and followed the line drawn by her finger to a distant wall of trees. No, not even then did I *dare* to believe that such a thing could be so.

It was windy when I left the house. A strong, early autumn cold front was coming through and rain was not far off. I had to shout my good-bye to be heard. "You better hurry," the widow Hancock said to my back, "if you're going to that swamp . . ."

There was more to that sentence, but the wind took the words from her mouth and scattered them.

"I've been wet before," I said, turning, waving. And before I reached the edge of the woods, I was wet again.

No, I didn't give the venture much hope; can't say I was even seriously looking as I navigated the old logging road that bisected the swamp. Until a small yellow rain-dampened bird, which must have been sitting on a branch right in front of me, flushed, flew, and disappeared behind a wall of Atlantic white cedar.

I don't know how many of you have ever seen a white cedar

swamp. The trees stand as thick as fur and the needles absorb all sunlight. The air is heavy and close; the water, tannin-stained and still. The bottom is *treacherous,* log-strewn. Slick with slime and the underlying muck has no equal this side of a basketball hoop.

I plunged in after the bird and jockeyed for two hours to get a look at the creature. Twice I caught a glimpse of a slim yellow form maneuvering around trunks. Once, from a distance, I saw it perched—or saw *something* perched that might have been, *must* have been, the bird.

Even from a distance, it was clear that it wasn't a flycatcher—not an empid flycatcher, anyway. The stance was more horizontal than erect. The silhouette slim. The tail twitchless. The head? Small, warbleresque, maybe vireolike.

You know, Wilson lumped vireos, flycatchers, and even some of the warblers together—calling them *all* flycatchers.

The bird never vocalized. Never.

I cannot tell you what this bird was. I can only tell you what it was not, and THAT is what brought me back the next morning—with chest waders and a camera and an optimism that could not be realized. The bird wasn't there—had probably gone with the front, migrated south. I went back several more times in the next couple of weeks, but it made no difference. The yellow bird that shed all the bird names I knew (except one) was gone.

Disappointed? Oh yes! Devastated. But you know the disappointment didn't last. It gave way to a secret, maybe a selfish, sort of elation. Because, you know, I *had* seen this bird. Really seen it! Not definitively. Not backed up by any evidence. But *seen* what the old Quaker gentleman had seen—and no one else since Wilson and Audubon. SEEN! What *had* to be. What couldn't be anything *but* . . . a small-headed flycatcher.

Why, it was the greatest ornithological rediscovery since Gurney's pitta (whatever the hell that is). Might be the ornithological discovery of the century.

My discovery (now that the Quaker was dead). Mine!

And to prevent hordes of people from descending on the spot and threatening the safety of the bird, I . . . uh . . . decided to say nothing about its existence or its whereabouts to anyone.

Anyone! Including, maybe *particularly,* the widow Hancock. Lord only knows who she might blab to.

Anyone!

Remember what happened between Audubon and Wilson: disputed claims, muddied glory. Remember what happened to the last great auks on the planet? They were collected. Remember what has happened to a host of birds from ivory gulls coming to feeders in New York State to assorted exotic hummingbird species along the Gulf Coast? Captured, banded, released, and never seen again.

So I decided not to take a chance—not to breath a word of the bird's existence to a living soul—until I could secure photographic evidence of my discovery when the small-headed flycatcher returned in the spring.

Listen. A digression. I hate to break up a good story line, but I've got to tell you this. A funny thing happened to me the day after I discovered the bird and went back again. I met this odd-looking kid about eight or nine years old. He was wearing grimy shorts and a Grateful Dead T-shirt. His face was dirty. He needed a haircut. He was sitting on the hood of my car.

At first I thought it was the dirt on his face that made him look so odd, but as I got closer I realized that it was the face *itself* that was odd. The features were crooked, out of place. The lips thin, almost absent. Nose small, pushed to one side. Ears large and asymmetrical—one sat high and forward, the other was low, trailing behind the jaw.

And the eyes? The eyes were wide and staring, and they seemed to be focused upon something far, far away.

You will understand that New Jersey's bay shore is an isolated place and that blood has been mixed here over and over again. Heredity thickens and clots in places like the Delaware bay shore—genes unravel and sometimes children are born whose bodies or minds are misshapen and bent, sometimes both.

"You need a haircut," I said, trying to sound friendly, trying to bend his gaze my way.

"I live in that house," he said, pointing, turning his head (but not his gaze) toward the sound of my voice.

The house was old, mantled by towering sycamores with trunks as rotten as the structure.

"That's a nice house," I said, putting a patch over the obvious poverty with a lie. "What's your name?"

"My dad's lame up," he replied.

"Oh, that's too bad," I said. "Did he have an accident?"

"Our yella lab just had pups, an' one is mine for keeps."

"That's terrific," I said (beginning to wonder whether the kid had even one oar in the water). "What are you going to name it?"

"We got a television," he replied—another digression, not the name of the dog.

"Ah, what's your favorite program?" I probed, but without much optimism. The kid was definitely on the outside looking in.

"What's them," he said, turning his face and a finger my way again. The finger fell on my binoculars.

"Binoculars," I said, but the name evidently meant nothing to him. "They make the world look bigger."

The kid didn't say anything for a while—nothing at all—and I thought, "I've lost him completely." Until I realized that the eyes that would not focus were fastened upon the binoculars. Then they went flat again.

"No," he said.

"Oh yes," I insisted. "Here, I'll show you." I held the binoculars up to his eyes, set them for infinity, and directed them across the marsh toward a cargo ship moving up the shipping lane in the bay . . . on past a series of duck blinds . . . over toward a harrier hunting the marsh.

He didn't move his hand to hold them. In fact, except for his head, he didn't move at all. And when I took the binoculars back he turned, and without another word he walked away.

Two days later, when I returned to search again for my flycatcher, he was there waiting, and a week later he came running out as soon as my car came into view. We never did exactly hit it off conversationally. But he followed me around, offering me the benefit of his disjunct thoughts, and he looked through my binoculars every chance he got.

The last time I went to the swamp, sometime during the first week in September, I surprised him with a present. A pair of Swarovski 8×30 binoculars on loan to me for review. I was supposed to return them. I told the public relations people I lost them.

I gave him a field guide too. One of Roger Peterson's. I would have given him a National Geo guide, but I didn't think he was advanced enough for subspecies differentiation yet.

The kid just stood there holding the binoculars in one hand and the book in the other, staring at whatever it was that he stared at beyond the horizon. Then he said good-bye.

I wondered how he knew.

It was a long winter, a long time to wait for the ornithological rediscovery of the century. I gave Linda a new camera and telephoto flash system for Christmas (then played with the stuff through Christmas dinner, focusing over and over again on a Wilson lithograph hanging on the wall).

I spent countless hours staring at the ceiling in January, out the window in February, wondering where small-headed flycatchers winter. Wondering how the species had survived, *could have* survived, for so long undiscovered in a small, well-birded state.

It was the cedars, of course—that was the key! Atlantic white cedar is, as it was two centuries ago, a coveted wood: straight-grained, rot-resistant, easy to work, wonderfully scented. Decoys were carved from it, ships' masts fashioned, chests built, closets lined. The shingles of Liberty Hall in Philadelphia, home of the Continental Congress, were cut in Dennisville, New Jersey, you know.

And after the greed for white cedar had stripped the trees from the land, why, they mined for it. Plumbed the depths of clear-cut swamps, raising still-perfect logs from the muck, though some had lain there for centuries.

It was a perfect explanation—a flycatcher that lived in white cedar stands! The habitat was destroyed. The bird disappeared. And now, after a century of regeneration (New Jersey is 45 percent forested, you know), there were once again maturing stands of white cedar in the state . . . *and a small-headed flycatcher!* Somewhere, somehow, the bird had survived.

Over the course of the winter I read everything I could about Alexander Wilson, bored cocktail party guests to tears with the nuances of his life. I even wrote to Alex Trebek on *Jeopardy*, suggesting that they include an Alexander Wilson category on the show.

I hung Wilson's portrait in my room, studied the fragile face and tannin-dark eyes, and practiced in the mirror until I had the look down pat. Then in January I went to Bacharach's and had my portrait taken—you know, for press purposes, for when I broke the news of the discovery in the spring.

I could see it. Me and Al Wilson (and maybe J. J. Audubon too), side by side, front-page news. I could read the headlines . . .

In the *New York Times:* ORNITHOLOGICAL ENIGMA SOLVED IN SWAMPS OF SOUTH JERSEY: 180-YEAR-OLD RIFT BETWEEN OR-NITHOLOGICAL GIANTS MENDED BY AUDUBON NATURALIST.

In the *New York Daily News:* DUNNE DOES IT: DISCOVERS DIS-PUTED DICKYBIRD.

In the *National Enquirer:* EXTINCT SWAMP CREATURE USES TIME WARP TO REAPPEAR IN 20TH CENTURY. "It turned my boy into a birdwatching zombie," tearful mother relates.

Then, early in March, on a day with southwest winds pushing clouds across the sky and daffodils poking through the shroud of last year's leaves, I journeyed to South Philadelphia, to Gloria Dei (also known as Old Swedes' Church), the place where the father of American ornithology lies.

I found the grave easily enough. Read the inscription on the monument. Ran my fingers over the letters of the barely legible name etched in stone and told the stone, and whatever spirit it housed, the secret I could not reveal to a living soul.

Then I journeyed uptown to the College of Physicians, the institution that George Ord, Wilson's biographer, companion, and friend, left his papers to. I went to the ancient card files, flipped through the names, wrote a stack number on a form, and turned it over to a librarian. Ten minutes later the sleeves of my sport jacket were smudged to the elbows with the dust and book mold of George Ord's copies of *American Ornithology*.

I didn't hurry my task. I leafed through the books, savoring the paintings, savoring them at random, savoring the genius of my secret sharer.

And in volume 6, plate L, figure 5, I found the painting that matched the one on our dining room wall, and on page 62 the text I sought *and the date*—the 24th of April—the day Wilson discovered the bird that was our bond.

The 180th anniversary of its finding was going to be a memorable one. Of this I was absolutely certain.

I don't remember what lies I told to free myself on that day. But I would have told anybody anything—anything but the truth, of course. And I don't remember anything of the ride—except for the last part. After I passed the Hancock House. And turned off the old Salem-Canton road. And rounded the corner. And saw the gaping hole in the wall of trees where the cedar swamp had stood. I can tell you everything that happened from that point on, which is strange because my mind was cold numb, and I remember it not as if it were something that really happened to me. I remember it the way you might recall a story told by a friend—the way you might recall this story to another.

The swamp was a sea of close-cut stumps; the water, thick with bark and branches. They'd cut it during the winter, of course, while the water was frozen. Cut all of it, just the way that people on the bay shore have cut timber for centuries.

There was a man. Wearing bibbed overalls and a John Deere cap. He was dragging logs with a tractor. I waved when he drew near, signaling him to stop, which he did by disengaging the clutch, leaving the engine running.

"*Have you seen a small-headed flycatcher?*" I yelled, trying to make my voice carry over the sound of the tractor.

"Ma Fly?" he said, looking down. Looking puzzled. Finding nothing amiss. Shaking his head to indicate he didn't understand. I tried again.

"*Have . . . Have you seen a small yellow bird?*" I pleaded, holding up two fingers. Hoping to offer dimensions (but I couldn't decide whether to show him the bird's length or its extent).

I'll give the guy credit. He tried. Leaned forward. Cupped a hand behind an ear. But it wasn't any use. He shook his head, pointed to his ear, grinned a toothless grin, and shrugged. Then he pointed to his watch, waved, and eased the tractor into gear.

I guess I stood there for a while. Just stood there. Then at some point I must have started walking. Thinking how it felt to let the ornithological find of the century slip through my fingers. Thinking that it could have been prevented.

Trying not to think of the fool I had been.

I don't know how far I walked—a mile, maybe two. And I don't know when the kid showed up, but suddenly he was there. Walking beside me. Being trailed by a yellow labrador retriever. And he was chattering about something. Some stupid bird or another.

"How are things at home?" I intoned.

"A big ol' bird," he said, sticking to the subject. "Bigger'n a crow, big as a hawk but . . ."

"How's your father's leg?" I interrupted, not caring one way or the other.

"*Black!* Not brown," he said continued. "*Real* black! And *white!* In the wings. Most especially when it flies an' . . ."

"Uh-huh. What'd you name the dog?"

"Its head's pointy and red on top," he continued, "(Leastwise, *one* of 'em is). An' the eye's all bright and shiny and butter-color . . . *like the bill.*"

"Mmmmm." I said. "Bill's a nice name for a dog. Seen anything good on TV lately?"

"An' they make *all* kinds o' noise," he said. "Bamming on wood and yappin' and everything. All the time! Especially near the tree they live in. In a hole. Down where the survey people were measurin'. For the new nuc-le-er electric plant they wanna build."

"Huh," I said. "I must have missed that program. Maybe I can catch it as a summer rerun."

The kid didn't say anything for a while. Just kept pace, looking up at me with those incredible blue eyes of his. Funny, you know I don't think I ever noticed the color before.

"I got to go now," he said suddenly, turning, waving, marching away. *Really marching.* He put his hand up to his mouth and started make tooting sounds—like he was blowing notes through a tin horn or something.

Cute kid. Nice dog.

That's about the end of the story. I wandered back to my car eventually. Drove to work. Went home that evening. When Linda asked me what was new, I told her the truth. "Nothing." Two hundred years had passed. Nothing had changed at all.

It did occur to me to write to the widow Hancock, to ask about any journals her husband might have kept. A couple of months later, I got a letter from a sister in Massachusetts, who told me the widow Hancock had passed away over the winter, that the estate had been sold, and that anything not salable, meaning paper and stuff, had been thrown away.

And no, I haven't been back to Greenwich, not since. Things like small-headed flycatchers, Bachman's warblers, heath hens, and . . . well . . . birds like these don't turn up every day. They are a once in a lifetime opportunity at best. I had my chance and I blew it.

But if *you* happen to be birding in South Jersey sometime soon, sometime next spring, you might want to wander on over to Greenwich and check it out. See what's around.

And if you happen to run into a blue-eyed kid with a faraway look in his eyes being followed by a good-looking lab the color of old ivory, Bill . . .

Tell him the guy who showed him how to make the world look bigger said "Hi."

DEEP POCKETS

When I was young, my wealth was stored in pockets. There was very little wealth in those days—not that much has changed—but what little I had fell neatly into those cotton-lined coffers. At bedtime the treasures would be extracted and lined up on the dresser so I could savor the favors of the day.

Some of this booty was perennial, the everyday objects that both distinguished me as me and bound me to the fraternity of pocket-packing youngsters. Principle among them was a wallet whose contents (a few photos and the odd letter or two) were mostly there for bulk. Prized was a Swiss Army knife whose array of accoutrements elicited wonder and envy among friends. Usually there was a pen, a Bic, and often as not it leaked.

Wedged between these perennial treasures were the special offerings of the season, the things picked up in my forays afield. In summer perhaps a good, smooth skipping stone found its way into pockets, or the shed skin of a garter snake. Winter forays might produce an owl pellet, a patch of rabbit fur discarded by a fox, or a bounty of praying mantis egg cases.

Important tip. If you go out collecting praying mantis egg cases, don't let them accumulate in the bottom drawer of your dresser. If you do, you'll learn something of insect development but more about a mother's wrath.

But spring and fall were the seasons when pockets ran full, the seasons when pockets fairly split at the seams. In April there were

Indian arrow points that germinated in newly plowed fields and, come May, a fresh crop of fishing lures dangled from overhanging limbs, challenging the most adventuresome hands.

Then autumn! With woodland trails marked with blue jay feathers and flicker feathers and hickory nuts and black walnuts and . . .

Acorns! Acorns so beautiful that they begged a hand to enfold them. Acorns so beautiful that every new one found eclipsed the beauty of the last and absolutely begged to join the others already crammed into pockets.

I am older now, and it strikes me as comfortably curious that in my forays afield I still measure wealth in terms of pockets. With binoculars and a stolen hour, I venture into a promising woodlot or an old familiar haunt in search of roving pockets of birds. In winter, these include perennials like chickadees and titmice, creepers and downy woodpeckers—birds I know I'll always find there.

But in spring and fall, other species fill out these woodland pockets, giving form to the season and impetus to the search. Yellow-rumped warblers and black-and-whites, animate redstarts and buzzy-voiced bluewings, Blackburnian warblers of the impossibly beautiful raiment and black-throated blues—my perennial favorite. Each seems more beautiful than the last, and they find a place in the pockets of my mind to be carried home.

In the evening, when the lights are out and I sink between the sheets, snug as a penknife in a pocket, I dig into the coffers of my mind and review the treasures of the day. Giving each treasured glimpse its due, anticipating the birds that may be gathered into pockets tomorrow.

EMBERS OF SPRING

Winter, when the Christmas counts have passed, when snow has lost novelty and turned to slush, recalls to me a fireplace after the logs have been reduced to ash. Walking through some landscape, I contemplate the essence of an extinguished season but find myself looking ahead toward the blaze of light and life called spring. Red-winged blackbirds are the embodiment of this season-vaulting exercise.

With their coal-colored bodies and smoldering shoulders, they seem like the embers I find when I sift through the ashes of yesterday's fire, searching for a spark to ignite another blaze. Their presence in December and January assures me that winter never quite conquers. Their display, on that first warm morning in February, proves that winter is finite.

The way I mark my calendar, spring arrives the day the epaulets flare.

You know the day the moment you step from the car. There is something in the air—some spark, perhaps, as opposing seasons are struck together. There is something about the way the birds comport themselves, something that sets them apart—or maybe it is just that the birds themselves are set apart, spread like ink spots across a muslin-colored landscape where before they'd gathered in flocks.

On wind-whipped shrubs or winter-beaten reeds the birds hitch themselves aloft. Bouncing in the breeze, holding their ground when approached, the birds return the question in your eyes with a beady stare.

For minutes on end, nothing happens. The birds stand like actors who have forgotten their lines, each waiting for the next to offer the cue. Finally one bird begins the ritual that breaks winter's spell.

Boldly it arches its back. Theatrically it drops its head. Imploringly it droops its wings. Then, chanting the magic incantation that turns winter into spring, it flares its epaulets, sending a red-and-yellow spark streaking across the landscape.

"Tur-a-ling."

A rival catches the spark and, mimicking its neighbor's movements, makes its own epaulets blaze. Another bird bursts into color and song. Another . . . another . . . until the whole marsh blazes with wind-fanned embers.

Other places boast other first signs of spring. Crows that stream north over snow-covered landscapes. Vees of waterfowl that drive a wedge into winter. Spiraling woodcock that dance themselves dizzy. Small frogs that force spring's door open with a resonant *"cre e e ek."*

But for me, for as long as I can remember, the herald of spring has been the coal-colored bird with the ember-colored epaulets. The blackbird that springs from an ash-colored world, igniting the coming season with an ember from the last.

Part 4

. . . AND

BIRDING

GETTING A LEG UP
ON BIRD-SIGHTING SHEETS

Without a sideways glance my dog, Moose, gained the fire hydrant and began his standard olfactory analysis. Starting low, working up along the hydrant's length, he reviewed the passing and the fortune of his fellow canines.

Sometimes his focus was arrested by a particularly poignant entry. His nose would pause and ponder. Sometimes his nose would interpret something that rated a derisive sniff, and he'd move on quickly. Finally, his analysis completed, Moose saluted the post with a raised rear paw, adding his name to the list.

That's when it hit me. I've seen this behavior before—and so have you. It's a near universal practice among birders. It's called checking the bird-sighting sheet.

It happens every day in open-air pavilions and visitor centers all across the country: set-jawed birders stalk toward the clipboard marked "Recent Bird Sightings" and study the entries. Starting with the most recent sightings, working back, they run their fingers along the list, gleaning the fortune of birders who'd passed this way before them.

Chancing upon a noteworthy sighting claimed by a birder whose pedigree is uncertain, they sniff. Discovering that some other top dog has beaten them to print on a good bird, they bristle.

And when the review is completed, the birders each get to make their mark. They raise a pen and sprinkle the page with hot new entries—to post notice of their passage, to offer testimony of their skill.

It's "D. Boone kilt a bar on this tree" with a birding spin. It's ritual posturing played out in the honest name of shared interest and free speech.

Most of the time these posturings are simple and straight-forward.

"*9/2/92. 5 buff-breasted sandpipers; 2 imm. Baird's Block C-5. B. Goodbirder.*"

"*3/15/93. Ad. m. Eurasian wigeon feeding in mixed flock east side of Ocean. Dr. I. C. Furst.*"

Sometimes entries are elaborate—actual dialogues between birders debating the merits and antimerits of an identification. (I recall a stint at New York's Jamaica Bay National Wildlife Refuge that touched off a war of words that consumed pages.)

Sometimes sighting sheets set the stage for real-life drama. Several years ago, a verbal duel was played out on the pages of the bird-sighting sheet at a birding hot spot in South Texas. At issue was one of the most fundamental tenets of birding: shared information.

On one side of the issue stood several local birders who were logging directions to a roosting long-eared owl (a local rarity). They were exercising the right of free speech. On the other side was the individual who had, in fact, discovered the bird and who was leading people to the site for pay. He was exercising the right of free enterprise (and carefully excising written directions to the bird with a pen).

Free speech versus free enterprise, but the dispute was settled by an act of free will: the bird left (leaving the issue very much unresolved).

Not all the information imparted in bird-sighting sheets is informative or even valid. In fact, some of the things that find their way into print don't even relate to birds.

For example, the knee-jerk notations of people who can't distinguish bird-sighting sheets from visitor logs.

"*John and Mary Pseudonym. Just visiting. Lovely park.*"

For example, the trite musings of feeble-minded individuals who use bird-sighting sheets to demonstrate how clever they are.

"Woody Woodpecker. Identified by call. Ha-ha-ha HA-ha."

Oh, I'll admit that some of the feathered fictions that find their way into sighting logs brush the limits of the clever registry. Despite its latitude, Cape May Point State Park, New Jersey, enjoys a rash of penguin sightings every summer. Visiting birders are startled by this—until they realize that the park's beach is adjacent to Saint Mary's by the Sea, a summer vacation retreat for Roman Catholic nuns.

Birding's ethic of honesty prevents *real* birders from resorting to creative chicanery of this nature—except, perhaps, during competitive Big Days when a "ghost" pectoral sandpiper, strategically plotted, can cause rival teams to waste lots and lots of time.

The ethic also does not extend to several wry-minded surrogates of my acquaintance who travel the country, attaching my moniker to sightings like "Canada goose" (a bird I actually like) and "Sea gull" (regrettably, a bird I've never seen).

Fact is, I only wish I could travel as widely as my name. Fact is, my signature is illegible. Hint to readers: if you can read the signature in the bird-sighting book, it's not me.

My favorite all-time notation in a bird-sighting log was anonymous. It didn't even relate to any particular bird. It celebrated an event.

It was a Memorial Day weekend, the closing days of spring. Migration had been poor, some said nonexistent, and mornings came and went without the fallout everyone dreamed of.

Then, on Saturday morning, birders up and down the eastern seaboard woke up to an avalanche of birds, a tidal wave of color and song. No mere list of sightings could do justice to that day. But one birder managed to summarize the spectacle that could not be itemized.

In letters that spanned two pages of the log, the birder wrote: THIS IS IT!

And that, so simply and eloquently put, was that.

CONFESSIONS OF
A LISTING HERETIC

Birding (like civilization) is founded upon adherence to common standards and practices. It's what distinguishes us from the savages: from golfers, from people who cheat at solitaire. It's what makes life lists and Big Day scores and Christmas bird counts possible, comparable year to year, team to team, person to person.

What would we have if some people went around spuriously counting red-legged black ducks as full species and other people just up and decided that black ducks and mallards were conspecific?

Anarchy. That's what.

Would you want to bring up a young birder in a world where some people counted green kingfishers seen on the Mexican side of the Rio Grande or even *lied* about the birds they counted on their life list?

You would not!

On the other hand, there's a lot of gray out there between the black and white. Some of the rules governing what and how birds are counted are hard and fast. Others are open to interpretation. And sometimes even the most conscientious birders have been known to hedge just a wee little bit in the name of a good bird or a good cause. In fact, some of my favorite birders have advocated positions with regard to the legitimacy of certain birds that are downright heretical.

Take, for example, Dr. Ernest Choate, who was for many years Cape May's birder laureate and the keeper of the Cape May bird list. For years, Ernie carried a Manx shearwater on the Cape May bird list, even though the bird was seen off the Lewes, Delaware, breakwater—twelve miles from Cape May. His rationale: "We can count anything on the Cape May list that can be seen from shore. On a clear day, we can see Lewes, Delaware. Therefore we can count the bird."

This same brand of logic has led my good friend Clay Sutton to practice a most convincing reinterpretation of the rules governing Christmas bird count circles. The northern limit of the Cape May count passes through Goshen. From Goshen an observer can see Jake's Landing three miles away, and if you are gifted with the eyes and skills of Clay Sutton, you can even see and identify hunting raptors at that distance. But for the sake of accuracy, Clay makes it a point to go over and "ground-truth" his observations.

Maybe it's the spirit of the season, but Christmas bird counts tend to bring out the loose interpretationist in us all. Nobody will ever know how many count circles are dotted with "pimples"— little bulges in those pure-hearted lines that sneak into key locations. Why, the venerable Barnegat CBC has half of Long Beach Island dangling off its southern rim—a veritable geographic hemorrhoid! And, in the best tradition of Christmas counts, some of the birds that get reported at the roundups would prompt Diogenes to blow his brains out.

I'm a practicing and self-avowed listing heretic myself, and this is what gives me standing to throw stones. Once, on the Walnut Valley Christmas Count, I went out for a bit of predawn owling. A heavy snow had fallen overnight, stopping just after two in the morning. Traveling down the road (of course, *in* the count circle!), my headlights picked up something lying on the road. Closer examination disclosed a dead screech owl. The bird was lying fully atop the snow. *Therefore* it had been killed after two o'clock. *And therefore* it had been alive and in the count circle on the count day.

Screech owl. Check.

And then there was the black vulture claimed by the Guerrilla Birding Team in the 1988 World Series of Birding. The bird was nesting in a cave well out of our route. A nocturnal visit was the only alternative, but there didn't seem to be any way to approach the cave without frightening and maybe flushing any adult within—something we patently refused to do. Midnight found me fifty feet from the cave entrance, playing a flashlight in the trees above the cave, hoping vainly to find the bird at roost. Just as I was preparing to leave, a loud "hisssss" emanated from the cave entrance. I left. With a smile.

Black vulture by call. Check.

This same spirit of concern is what led to an impromptu rule change in this year's World Series of Birding. A very accessible goshawk nest had become known to many of the event's participants, and concern for the bird's welfare mounted. To save the bird from harassment, a ruling was made. Any team that knew the location of the nest needed only drive to the grove, park, wait three minutes, then drive away. The bird would count, sight unseen.

But the finest example of creative counting I have ever heard of is credited to the venerable Floyd P. Wolfarth, who once while hawk watching saw a distant flock of brant suddenly break into two flocks, one of which disintegrated into chaos. His conclusion: only two birds could have precipitated such a reaction—a golden eagle or a gyrfalcon. An eagle would have been visible at that distance; a gyr, no. Therefore . . .

And at the end of the fall, when the Raccoon Ridge totals were posted. There it was too. In black and white.

FORMULA FOR
A WHITE-WINGED TERN

Seeing a white-winged tern, Old World marsh tern, and New World waif is not an easy matter, certainly not as easy as just heading for Delaware's coastal marshes in late July, scanning the flocks for *Chlidonias* terns, and picking out the one with the pale white rump. Oh no! Finding the white-winged tern takes luck or skill or perseverance—or, usually, all three!

But for white-winged tern aspirants who are neither lucky, skilled, nor patient, there is another way to get the bird. It relies on a sure-fire formula: a set of conditions that once met virtually guarantee success. In fact, so foolproof is this formula that practitioners might just as well (and just as legitimately) simply check off the bird and stay home.

To get the white-winged tern, pick a day when the temperature and the humidity make the air feel like chowder and the only shade around lies beneath a cloud of mosquitoes. You must be sure to wear shorts, so as not to encumber the catalytic chomp of greenhead flies, and to leave your baseball cap in the car (next to your water bottle, insect repellent, and lunch), so the biting deerflies can inject madness into your method.

The choice of vantage point is critical. You must stand on the far side of the largest impoundment pool—as far from the flocks of feeding terns as possible and still be able to count the bird in Delaware. Make sure that the sun is directly in your eyes. If you can see color or distinguish shape through the glare, move to a worse location.

It helps to have poor optics—binoculars so out of alignment that they would induce eyestrain in a potato, a spotting scope so internally fouled that the world looks like it's been lacquered with mustard. It also helps to have a field guide that assures you that the bird is unmistakable within *range* and *habitat*. (Since you will be relying on "giz" to confirm your identification, you will certainly be within range; and, since you followed the directions given on the hotline, you will unquestionably be in the right habitat.)

It is also important to surround yourself with white-winged tern aspirants who are as desperate for the bird as you are.

People who need it for their seven hundredth North American life bird or who are trying to break the Delaware Big Year record.

People who own $3,400 spotting scopes and talk about how they've seen *leucopterus* on three continents (yet are never seen to scan).

People who flew in from California, have searched for three futile days for "the bird," and must fly out that night.

People who are "absolutely certain" that they saw "the bird" earlier in the day but who came back hoping for a "better look." Saw it . . .

"Here?"

"Right here?"

"Close?"

"As close as those birds are now. Close enough to count. But, you know, I'm the kind of birder who really likes to study their life birds, not just count them the way some people do—know what I mean? That's why I came back, hoping . . ."

It helps to have a number of birders present who still need seaside sparrow for a life bird (to help inflate the confidence levels of serious white-winged tern aspirants). It is essential that Kenn Kaufman *not* be present, so that serious WWT aspirants will not be intimidated by an expert presence.

If all the elements are as I have described them, then conditions are conducive for finding a white-winged tern, *but* there is still one element missing. The formula for finding a white-winged tern demands that you time your visit to coincide with that period when juvenile Forster's terns are capable of sustained flight—Forster's terns that show dark backs, white rumps, dark caps, and a shallow forked tail just like a basic plumage . . .

"WHITEWINGEDTERN! In the flock! Going right. Going left. Going right."

"Is it still going left?"

"Right!"

"*Got it!*"

"Got it!"

"Got *it!*"

"Got it!"

That's *definitely* the bird I had this morning."

So, if you follow this formula as stated, if you want to see a white-winged tern badly enough, success is guaranteed. It's either this or wait until a real white-winged tern passes close enough to note definitive field marks.

But like I said, that takes luck or skill. And who has time for that?

THE PRICE OF RESPECTABILITY

He was wearing a leprous white panama, lizard skin shoes, and a platinum-colored suit that glistened like a shark in a sauna. He was stepping out of a limo the color of a cherub's bottom and the size of a luxury liner.

"It's the fifty-pound sterling silver swan on the hood that makes it," I thought. But that was before I noticed the light-rimmed vanity plate that read (I swear I'm not making this up) "John."

While the gas station attendant rushed to fill it up, one of the planet's seamiest denizens began eyeballing my car, phonetically decoding the legend emblazoned across the hood that read "New Jersey Audubon Society." Fixing what I read to be a patronizing smile upon me, the man identified as John strutted to my open window, pointed to the New Jersey Audubon logo, and said more than asked: "You one of those *bird*watchers?"

"At last," I thought nostalgically. "A member of society who wants to demean me." It's been a long time since anyone has been disparaging about my avocation, and frankly I miss my old social misfit standing.

Half a lifetime ago, birdwatching was an interest you hid in the closet. If you were a kid, it wasn't cool; it was certain to get you picked last when they divvied up sides for sandlot baseball. If you were an adult, it made you tantamount to a commie sympathizer, might even have landed you in jail (particularly if you espoused a liking for prothonotary warblers).

I can remember my parents discussing my unnatural attraction to birds and wondering how to replace the binoculars in my hands with something more socially acceptable, like a baseball bat. I can remember telling a guidance counselor that I liked watching birds— and being called back for extra sessions.

Even after I grew up, went to college, started working for New Jersey Audubon, I *still* couldn't earn the social acceptance accorded your average mass murderer. When family and friends would ask my brothers what Pete was doing, they'd mumble something inaudible and change the subject. One poignant evening I described all the neat bird-related stuff I was engaged in to my sainted grandmother, only to be treated to her admonition: "You should have stayed in the carpet business—you'd be making good money now."

There was some stigma associated with being a birdwatcher, some shame (or pride) that divided the world up between us (birders) and them (society's rank and file). Birding made you an outcast, a renegade. Over time not only did I come to accept a measure of social severance, I grew to like it.

"Heck," I reasoned, "if everybody liked watching birds there'd be gridlock on the refuge auto routes and standing room only on the hawk watch."

That's all changed now. Suddenly everybody's into birding and everybody wants to know about it. When the whiskered tern set down in Cape May for a North American first, network newscasters were calling and begging for interviews. Now that it has become established that birders are an economic force, optics manufacturers are pleading for marketing tips, and every whistle-stop chamber of commerce is planning a birding festival.

Whenever I drive somewhere in the company car, people wave, flash membership cards in assorted environmental organizations, stop me in parking lots, and ask how to attract hummingbirds. Worried parents ask me how to get the video joysticks out of their kids' hands and replace them with binoculars.

Suddenly I'm not an outcast anymore. I'm a personality. An oracle. An avenue to spiritual enlightenment and economic development. Suddenly everyone wants to tell me about the house finch nesting over their hot tub, or the product they've developed that keeps squirrels off of feeders.

Suddenly, after a lifetime of being a social outcast, I'm normal. And I can't stand it. I feel like Dostoyevsky without his guilt, Ahab without out his whalebone leg, King Richard without his hump. That is why I greeted John's approach so gleefully. Here, I felt certain, was a man who could give me back my hump.

"Why, yes," I assured the lizard-shod gentleman. "I'm a birder."

"Oh, man, that's wonderful," he said, destroying all hope for a testy exchange. "I got a question for you. See, I love birds. And every morning I go to this parking lot to feed the sea gulls. Whenever my car pulls into the lot, the birds just crowd all around me. Now, what I want to know is, do you think they really recognize me or what?"

"Sir," I said, taking in both the figure and the car, "I'm confident they recognize you."

"Oh, that's just wonderful," he said. "By any chance does your organization accept charitable donations?"

"I should have stayed in the carpet business," I thought.

ETERNAL ERRORS

"Hello," the somewhat hopeful voice intoned. "I'm with the [she gave the newspaper's name], and I'm calling about . . ."

"The photo on the cover of your bird festival insert that's labeled a double-crested cormorant but is in reality a male anhinga?"

"Then it's true?" she asked.

"We've been laughing about it all morning," I said cheerfully.

"Oh NOOOOOoooo," the voice more or less wailed, and I could certainly appreciate the person's discomfiture. After all, a bird publicly misidentified is a momentary embarrassment. But boo-boos that get set in print—well, published boo-boos are forever.

Sometimes the root of these offset (mis)identifications is simple ignorance—like the anhinga photo signed off by an editor on the staff, or like the illustration that accompanied the ad for the Cordova Shorebird Festival in 1993.

Intrigued by the festival's choice of an apparent thick-knee, as opposed to a shorebird species more representative of coastal Alaska, I phoned the Cordova Chamber of Commerce to gain insight into the selection process.

"Oh, we have them here," a very friendly voice assured.

"I don't think so," I said.

Her assurance undermined, the chamber representative said she would talk to the ad's designer and get back to me, which she did.

"Yes," she announced. "We have them here."

"Have what?" I asked.

"Curlews," she said.

"Yes," I agreed, finally understanding. "Bristle-thighed curlews, 'Hudsonian' curlews, but not *stone* curlews. That's an Old World species."

"Oh," she said.

Sometimes the boo-boos are rooted not in ignorance but in a moment's carelessness. One of my favorite faux pas involved an article in an eastern Pennsylvania newspaper extolling the merits of the year's osprey migration at famed Hawk Mountain Sanctuary.

"One of the best migrations in memory," the columnist said. *"Evidence that the birds are making a comeback."*

All this was verifiably so. The discord had nothing to do with the copy but with the photo accompanying the article—a photo which I carefully (and gleefully) clipped and sent to my friend and then Hawk Mountain curator, Jim Brett, along with the observation that the year's osprey migration was probably among the latest on record as well as the finest—provided the head shot of the adult northern goshawk accompanying the article was representative of the "osprey" they'd been counting.

Funny, but until that photo I'd never really noticed how similar the facial patterns of adult goshawks and ospreys really are.

I've been party to a few printed indiscretions myself, of course. Among the finest was an article penned about the Salton Sea, in which I habitually referred to yellow-*legged* gulls instead of the indigenous yellow-footed gulls.

But my all-time prize-winning misprint was the mess-by-committee blunder committed against the first edition of *Hawks in Flight*. At the page proof stage, coauthors Clay Sutton, David Sibley, and I noted that the illustration covering large falcons—peregrine and prairie falcons—had been mislabeled, a problem we attempted to correct with a call to the publisher. The gremlins won anyway. When the book was published, not only were the prairie and peregrine falcons still mislabeled, so was the gyrfalcon.

Perhaps the most hilarious insult to accuracy I have ever witnessed related not to an article but to a video. A birdseed company, hoping to secure an endorsement from the American Birding Association, sent a promo tape that was aired at a meeting of the association's board of directors. At one pregnant moment, a point-blank male house finch was shown that, to everyone's astonishment, threw back its head and belted out a beautiful morning warbler song.

Needless to say, the members of the board almost collectively ruptured their diaphragms. Needless to say, the company did not secure an endorsement.

Back to the anhinga.

"It's no big deal," I assured the distraught young caller. "These things happen all the time."

"Oh, but it *is* a big deal!" she said. "The contest rules state that only photos taken in Cape May County [New Jersey] are eligible. And anhingas aren't found in Cape May County, are they?"

"Not commonly," I agreed.

"But sometimes," she said, grasping the short straw.

"Yes, sometimes," I confirmed. "There are several records for the county."

"Then the photographer *could* have taken the picture here?"

I didn't say anything for a moment. I thought about saying yes. Then I thought about saying nothing. Then I told her the truth.

"Not likely," I said. "The bird is sitting in a mangrove tree, and mangroves aren't native to Cape May either."

"OOOOoooo," she said.

PASSING SIGHTS AND SOUNDS

[*Scene: A small parking lot serving a popular coastal birding area best known for autumn migrants. It is midmorning. The cars are thinning. Parking spaces that would have been filled instantly an hour earlier now stand vacant.*

Two birders approach each other from opposite ends of the lot. One is in his early fifties. His walk is brisk, his manner relaxed, open, friendly. His clothes look like they were lifted right out of the pages of "Town and Country" magazine, and his 10×42 binoculars are so new that the strap squeaks. With the touch of a button on his key ring, a silver Range Rover blinks its lights and chirps a greeting. The other man is younger, in his early twenties. His face is intense but calm, his eyes translucent and alert. He needs a haircut. He is wearing old jeans and a faded World Series of Birding T-shirt. Around his neck hangs a pair of ancient binoculars held together with duct tape. His bicycle is chained to the fence next to the Range Rover. He bends down to unfasten the chain just as the other man arrives.]

OLDER BIRDER. Hello! How's the birding?

YOUNGER BIRDER. [*Looking up, nodding*] Hello. [*Pauses, listening or maybe just thinking before he answers*] The birding's fine.

OLDER BIRDER. Terrific. Great morning. Got three year birds today: merlin, Cape May warbler, and a gray-cheeked thrush. How about you?

YOUNGER BIRDER. [*Still bent over, spinning the dial on his combination lock*] A lot of early season neotropical migrants are still going through, but blackpoll and palms arrived in good numbers. Some middle-distance stuff turned up as well. Eastern phoebe, white-throats, kinglets. [*Pauses, thinking*] Lots of thrushes dropping in early.

OLDER BIRDER. Sounds great. Gray-cheeked is a real prize, you know. Couldn't have gotten it without these. [*Points to his binoculars*] Unbelievable bins. Crystal clear! Have you seen them yet? They're new.

YOUNGER BIRDER. [*Not looking up, still concentrating on his bicycle lock*] Yes.

OLDER BIRDER. [*Taking off his binoculars, offering them*] Go ahead. Try them. [*The younger birder stands, takes the binoculars, examines them, tries to hand them back.*] No. Go ahead. [*Smiles, encourages*] Look through them. You won't believe it. [*The younger birder obliges.*]

YOUNGER BIRDER. Nice. [*Starts to hand them back, hesitates. Looks up, searching the sky, then trains the binoculars on a trio of high-flying birds.*]

OLDER BIRDER. [*Looking up, squinting*] Swallows?

YOUNGER BIRDER. Two Nashvilles and a palm.

OLDER BIRDER. [*Not listening*] Probably tree swallows. Wonderful glasses, aren't they?

YOUNGER BIRDER. [*Handing back the binoculars*] Yes.

OLDER BIRDER. [*Beaming*] Thanks. Knew you'd like them. I'm getting another pair for my wife. When we went to Antarctica last July her bins kept fogging. Ever been to Antarctica? Hell on equipment. You spend that much on a trip, you should have first-rate equipment.

YOUNGER BIRDER. No.

OLDER BIRDER. [*Startled*] What?

YOUNGER BIRDER. No. I've never been to Antarctica. You asked me.

OLDER BIRDER. [*At ease again*] Oh, right. Well, when you get to Antarctica, remember what I said about equipment. Don't cut corners.

YOUNGER BIRDER. [*Suddenly alert, searching*] Yellow-bellied flycatcher.

OLDER BIRDER. Did you say "Yellow-bellied flycatcher"? [*Younger birder nods but doesn't answer.*] Where?

YOUNGER BIRDER. I'm not sure. Somewhere in those trees over . . . [*Brings his binoculars up, a reflex as fast as a knee being assaulted by a hammer*] There it is. Perched in the sunlight . . . Flying now.

OLDER BIRDER. [*Bringing his binoculars up too late*] I didn't get on it. Why did you think it was yellow-bellied?

YOUNGER BIRDER. It called.

OLDER BIRDER. But you didn't see a yellow belly?

YOUNGER BIRDER. [*Hesitating*] No. It was an adult in very worn plumage.

OLDER BIRDER. [*Nodding sympathetically*] Too bad you didn't get a look at the belly. That's where quality optics really pay off. Like that gray-cheek this morning. Right in the shadows. Did you say you saw one too?

YOUNGER BIRDER. No. I said there were a lot of thrushes dropping in before dawn—mostly gray-cheeks and Swainson's.

OLDER BIRDER. It's tough telling gray-cheeks from Swainson's, isn't it?

YOUNGER BIRDER. [*Perplexed*] More from wood thrush, I think. Attenuation is sometimes a problem with distant gray-cheeks, but . . .

OLDER BIRDER. [*Breaking in*] Oh, wood thrushes are easy to tell from gray-cheeks. Much more spotting on the breast. Course, you need good optics. [*Looks at his watch*] Sorry, gotta run. Nice talking to you. Keep working on those thrushes. Takes practice.

[*The older birder gets in his car, closes the door, waves, then drives away. The younger birder watches for a moment, then bends down and finishes unlocking his bicycle.*]

MADE IN HEAVEN

The maitre d' stepped to our table, interrupting our exchange of greetings and introductions.

"The New York call you've been waiting for, madam."

"Please excuse me," the most beautiful woman in the world said, rising, leaving. She moved like a Roman goddess.

"What do you think?" Bob invited. "Isn't she wonderful."

"She is," I agreed. "But next time you meet a girl and decide to get married, give me and the airlines two weeks' notice or pick a best man on your side of the continent."

"What?" Bob said mockingly. "Not have the man who introduced me to birding supporting me at the altar. Unthinkable."

Bob and I go back a long way. Two bird-crazy kids who cut our teeth on Peterson. Though we hadn't seen each other since his move to the West Coast ten years earlier, it was clear Bob had lost none of his youthful exuberance. I knew, from correspondence and mutual friends, that he lived, breathed, and slept birding. Until now it had been his whole life.

"Where did the two of you meet?"

"At a desert rest area on I-10. There was a black-throated blue warbler reported."

"Sooo," I breathed in relief, "she's a birder?"

"A beginner," he affirmed.

"And you're her mentor."

"Sort of," he replied.

Bob must have noticed my look of perplexity because he added, "She doesn't know I'm a birder. When she backed into my car my binoculars were still under the seat."

"It wasn't her fault," he continued. "I sort of stopped behind her car when a *Dendroica* flew across the rest area."

"I see," I said, ignoring the chill running down my spine. "But she likes birds," I said hopefully.

"Of course!" Bob said (to my relief). "Why wouldn't she?" he added, ending that anxiety-free moment. My mind turned to the set of Stone's *Bird Studies at Old Cape May* I'd bought from an antique book dealer as a wedding present.

I was wondering whether it was too late to exchange them for a crystal punch bowl when Bob continued, "You don't think a Questar and Gitzo tripod combination is too heavy for someone weighing ninety-two pounds, do you? I'm afraid it might be," he added. "Especially when you add the weight of Sony TCD-D10 Pro II recorder and a Telinga parabolic mike."

"You bought her a Questar *and* a recording system for a wedding present!" I replied, trying to make it sound like a question (and failing).

"Of course," he said. "She's the love of my life. Besides, where we're going she'll need it. Go ahead," he demanded. "Guess."

"The Islands?" I offered.

"Island! Singular," he said.

"*The* Island?"

"The island," he affirmed. "Attu."

I tried to picture the moldy concrete bunker that houses Attu birders and apply the label "honeymoon suite," but without success. "Isn't Attu a little rustic for a . . . uh . . . beginning birder?" I cautioned.

"There's running water inside now," he said defensively.

"There's always been running water inside," I said.

"I mean in pipes," he said, piqued. "Anybody can go to Hawaii for a honeymoon. But how many people can say they went to Attu? Think about it."

I did think about it. And I blanched.

"Have you told her where you're taking her?"

"It's a surprise," he said.

"You are sure she's an outside sort of girl?" I ventured.

"I told you we met in a desert rest area. Stop worrying."

"Well, what's her profession . . . I mean does she . . ."

"She doesn't have to," Bob interrupted, clearly annoyed by my lack of enthusiasm. "She has family money generated by some international concern specializing in pharmaceuticals, entertainment, and transportation."

At this moment my questions were interrupted by the return of Bob's intended.

"What did your godfather say?" Bob asked anxiously.

The bride-to-be seemed momentarily unhappy—which, if anything, made her even more beautiful.

"I didn't speak with him," she said. "He's on a business trip to Central America. The call was from one of his, uh, lieutenants, who urged me to wait until Uncle gave his blessing before going through with the ceremony.

"But I said we are flying out tonight and that's all there is to it. I'm sure everything will be fine. I'm his favorite niece. He always says what makes me happy makes him happy.

"And," she giggled, reaching for her wine glass, looking into her lover's eyes, "what makes me unhappy, he makes disappear.

"Poof," she said, smiling secretly, tearing her eyes away from Bob and turning them upon me.

"Bob's told me so much about you, Pete. He said if there is anything not to like about him you are probably to blame.

"Incidentally," she added, "I gave my uncle's people your motel room in case there are any questions. I hope you don't mind."

"Excuse me," I said to the two of them. "I'll be right back." I lied.

FOR MELINDA

WITH LOVE AND SQUALOR

My biologist friend leaned across the car and opened the passenger seat door, dislodging an avalanche of Styrofoam cups, fermenting hoagie wrappers, pistachio shells, cassette tapes, and a well-seasoned, road-killed Virginia rail.

"So that's where that rail went," she said, grinning. "Just throw your gear anywhere," she invited, gesturing toward the rear—toward the pile whose components appeared to include half the contents of the library at Alexandria, elements of at least two mismatched tripods, a Bushnell Spacemaster spotting scope still being carried on some university's inventory, a cooler filled with benthic samples and long-neck bottles, a parachute, a sleeping bag, a pair of chest waders, the car's muffler, and two pairs of clogging shoes.

"Huh," I thought, hesitating, searching for an empty nook, "I didn't know Melinda was into clogging."

Melinda must have mistaken my hesitation for aversion. "Uh, sorry about the mess," she began, "but . . ."

"Don't mention it," I said, cutting her apology short, selecting a spot to toss my stuff that wouldn't topple the pile (or restrict access to the cooler). "My VW Rabbit is named Pig Pen," I explained.

"Oh," she said, smiling again, patting the dashboard of her Pinto sedan with obvious affection. "Pete, meet Detritus."

I'm not saying that all birders treat their cars the way Sherman treated Atlanta, or that the average birdingmobile looks like it was

lifted off the screen set for *The Grapes of Wrath*. I've known birders whose vehicles were so spotless they could serve as operating
rooms—birders who consider Windex and a portable vacuum as
indispensable as binoculars and spotting scope.

But most birders (at least most birders who grudgingly give me
access to their cars) have a more cavalier attitude about auto inte-
riors, and a good many of these acquaintances are plainly indifferent to them.

Consider Rick, a Maryland birder whose VW Golf looks like
it's been slept in—which it has, over and over again. During his
years as Maryland's breeding bird atlas coordinator, Rick has
probably logged more Z-time in his automotive steed than your
average small-town graveyard-shift patrol officer.

Consider Judy, from Mississippi. Judy's spunky Honda Civic is
a veritable automotive midden, filled with tokens and treasures
enough to humble the efforts of the most avaricious pack rat.

Consider my venerable old Pig Pen, whose deposition of
tracked-in debris was so thick come trade-in time that it had
formed geological strata. The top several layers were dry, desert-
like. But the underlying sediment, from middepth down to metal
core, had characteristics consistent with your basic Pleistocene
swamp.

My current steed, a Saab 900 (dubbed "Pete's Pit" by wife
Linda), is the latest in a proud line of dumpsters on wheels. Everything—I mean *every*thing—I might ever need in the next five years
is stashed in that car.

How do I know this? Because it has taken me five years to pro-
vision the Pit properly. Every time I went birding (shorebirding,
pelagic birding, hawk watching) and put some important accou-
trement (window mount, rain pants, lucky hawk-watching visor)
into the car, well, it just *stayed* there.

Say I'm birding Brigantine National Wildlife Refuge in July and
need an expedition-grade goosedown parka to save a fellow birder
whose air-conditioned rental has brought him to the brink of hy-
pothermia. Well, I've got one.

Say I run into Peter Matthiessen and want him to autograph a
copy of *Shorebirds of North America*. Well, I've got one of those

too. Found it just the other day while searching for a 40× eyepiece to fit the Balscope Senior I dropped off a jetty in 1974. It (the eyepiece) was located in the panel pocket of the 60/40 cloth jacket (I was wearing it the day I met Maurice Broun) that had unaccountably found its way into the duffel bag (containing my hiphugger bell-bottoms and work shirt embroidered with scenes inspired by *The Lord of the Rings*) instead of the old milk crate (that used to house my selection of eight-track tapes) where, of course, it belonged.

Small wonder it took so long to find it.

Now you are probably wondering why I just can't take all this stuff out of the car, store it at home, and draw upon it at need? Well, I certainly could! If I could predict when and where in July I was going to meet a hypothermic birder or run across a Balscope Senior in need of an eyepiece.

Or if home was a more orderly and organized place than my car—which it is not. As a matter of fact, if you *really* want to see chaos, you should see my office.

Makes what Sherman did to Atlanta look like urban renewal.

THE OLD MAN
AND THE PLOVER

He was an old man who birded alone, and he had gone eighty-four days now without finding a good bird.

"Cheer up," the boy had said. Before the fall term the boy had been his companion. Now they spoke only by phone.

"Remember we are in September," the boy continued.

"The month the good birds come," the old man said. "Anyone can be a birder in May—even you."

"Go suck an egg," the boy replied, but with humor. The old man had taught the boy to bird, and the boy loved him (even if the old man *did* still call northern harriers "marsh hawks").

"Tomorrow I will be at the dikes at dawn," the old man said. "To be there when the tide is full."

"Bitchin'," the boy replied. "Find something to make the members of the Records Committee commit suttee, old man."

"With luck," the old man replied.

He was there before the security gate opened. But he knew the trick of short-circuiting the electronic timer by placing a metal toolbox beside it so that it would open.

"I am an old man," he thought, "but I know many tricks."

He was well out on the dikes by the time the sun came up. With his binoculars, he scanned the pools.

"Just the usual stuff," he assessed. "Peep, yellowlegs, dows, stilts, and the odd pec." Then a falcon put the flocks up, and the old man saw the large dark-rumped plover for the first time.

"Yes," he said. "Yes." And he trained his scope on the place where the bird landed.

At first he saw nothing but the head, which was strangely shaped for golden plover. Then he saw the back, which was brightly spangled, and the underparts—black only to the legs and bordered by white.

"No," he said. "He can't be *that* good."

But he was that good, and the old man found a checklist, which was his only paper, and began sketching the details he could see.

"I wish I had the boy," the old man thought. The boy was an ornithology student who knew tertial talk and even the names of birds in scientific Latin.

Then he said aloud, "I wish I had the boy. To help me and to see this."

The old man had never seen a greater golden plover and could not recall all the field marks that distinguished it from the golden plovers of eastern North America. He illustrated what he saw, his hand cramping with the effort and his excitement, and was nearly finished when a falcon routed the bird for good.

"Have something?" a voice wanted to know.

The old man turned to see a stranger approaching. Everything about him was friendly except for the eyes, which were aloof.

"A greater golden plover in breeding plumage," the old man exclaimed. "You just missed it."

The stranger was silent, and his face now matched the eyes.

"Unlikely." he said. "There's one record for the lower forty-eight."

"Here," the old man offered, "my notes."

The stranger studied the sketch and handed it back.

"Looks like a *fulva*."

"What?"

"A *fulva*. Pacific golden plover. Don't you know that the lesser golden plover was split?"

The old man shook his head.

"Well, it was. You need to do some homework."

The old man was humiliated but not defeated, and he remembered the boy and how proud he would be, and so he resumed work on the sketch, recording the details now as he remembered them. It was then that he saw the next two birders approaching, members of the state Records Committee.

"*Ayy,*" he said aloud. There is no translation for this word, and perhaps it is just a noise such as a man might make, involuntarily, as his spotting scope goes over a jetty in a wind.

"Who else saw the bird?" the first one asked.

"Did you get photos?" the second one wanted to know?

"Did it call?" the first one demanded.

"Well, write it up anyway," they said before leaving.

"I should have brought a camera," he thought, sadly. "And I should have had the boy."

His hope was gone but not his pride. It wasn't until he returned to the refuge headquarters to log his sighting and was confronted by the assemblage of gripped birders that this, and all that was left of his happiness, was taken too.

"Did you notice the length of the legs?"

"Did you check the primary extension?"

"Did you note any signs of molt?"

"Did you see the color of the underwing lining?"

"Have you seen the species before?"

"Are you sure it wasn't just a black-bellied?"

In the end he did not log the sighting, and when the checklist with his diagram fell to the tarmac as he got into his car, he did not care.

Later a tourist couple taking a break from the casinos in Atlantic City made a wrong turn and wandered onto the refuge. The woman, seeing the paper, picked it up.

"What's that?" the man asked.

"A list of birds found on the refuge," the woman replied. "Someone's scribbled on it."

"I didn't know there were so many birds here."

"I didn't either," the woman replied.

"Maybe we should take up birdwatching. I'll bet it's fun."

"Maybe we should. It's got to be more fun than losing money."

At his home, the old man lay face down on the couch. He was sleeping without dreams and waiting for the boy to return his call. He wanted to say hello and to hear a friend's voice.

SEPARATING HOAGIES

We were sitting on the hawk watch eating hoagies—South Jersey subs. P.B.'s was a turkey and Swiss; mine was Italian with everything on it—not that you'd know this by simply looking at them. Hoagies are sort of the *Empidonax* flycatchers of the sandwich world.

"The Records Committee didn't accept your brown noddy sighting," P.B. confided, putting friendship ahead of procedure.

"Tooorifik," I said through a mouthful of salami/provolone/lettuce/tomato/pickles/hot peppers/extra oregano.

"You aren't upset?" he wanted to know.

"Nope," I assured, smiling grandly, going for another bite.

"Really?" he said.

"Really," I assured, savoring the last epicurean morsel.

P.B. paused, accepting the disclosure at face value. "Well, I wish other people were as understanding," he lamented.

I do too, for the sake of birders and records committee members alike.

Records committees have a difficult job. Their task: review sight records of unusual species and determine, on the basis of evidence, whether each record should or should not be added to the state's bird list.

The problem is, some birders regard records committees as judge and jury. The problem is, the acceptance or rejection of a sighting by a records committee is widely held to be a reflection upon the accuracy of the identification or the skills of the observer.

It is not. It cannot be. All a records committee can do is weigh evidence and determine whether it is sufficient to support acceptance. If a committee assumes authority more than this, it is overstepping its jurisdiction. If birders assume more than this, they are demeaning their own skills and responsibilities.

Look. It's simple. From bird to record book, a sighting has four levels of reality. First and most fundamental is *what the bird actually was*. If you believe in genetic coding, if you subscribe to the structured regimentation of Linnaeus, then you must believe that at some level all living things relate to nothing but one of their own kind.

Next, but not necessarily related, is *what the bird looked like—* which may or may not be the same as what it was. Molting plumage can transmute horned grebes into eared grebes; distance, heat waves, and an elevated perch can transform an Iceland gull into a great egret.

Now comes the human variable and level 3: *what the bird was identified as*. It might have been an Iceland gull and it might have looked like a great egret. But if an observer is confident that the bill was spatula-shaped . . .

Then comes the written description, based on notes and memory. Then comes the review by committee members who bring their cumulative experiences to bear. Then comes *what the committee believes*.

An observer is two steps removed from reality; the committee, three. Your reality as observer is more fundamental than theirs. You win on points. And while they, acting responsibly, may elect not to include the record on a state bird list, that does not and should not preclude you from including it on yours.

I tried to explain this to P.B., who listened intently but wasn't entirely won over by my philosophical equanimity.

"OK," I said. "Let's put it this way. What kind of hoagie did you have?"

"Turkey and Swiss," he said.

"On the basis of what evidence?" I demanded.

"That's what it tasted like," he asserted.

"I didn't taste it. What other evidence do you have?"

"It's what I ordered," he explained.

"You might have picked up the wrong sandwich at the counter," I suggested. "I need more evidence."

"The wrapper has a number 9 written on it," he pointed out. "Number 9 is turkey and Swiss."

"Wrapper isn't sandwich. The counterperson might have made a mistake."

"Well, I could give you a piece," he mused, "but it's all gone."

"So you can't. It's gone. And I reject your identification of turkey and Swiss on the basis of insufficient evidence."

P.B. looked puzzled, then exasperated. He started to say something but I cut him off.

"How did it taste?"

"It tasted great!"

"Then it doesn't make any difference whether I believe it or not, does it?"

"Not a bit," he said, smiling, pausing, reflecting, bringing the conversation back to where it started.

"You know," he said in all seriousness, "your bird could have been a black noddy instead of brown. It's possible."

"It could have been sliced chicken and not turkey."

"I would have known the difference," he promised.

And he would too.

NOSING OUT AN IDENTIFICATION. TAKING IT WITH SALT.

"Dr. Gesundheit to see you, Mr. Duster," the intercom intoned.

"Send him in," the editor of Hootin-Tootin's field guide series said, speaking into the book proposal clasped in his hands. Reaching the bottom of the page, registering no intrusion, he repeated the directive.

"I am in," a voice corrected.

"Oh," the editor replied, dropping the manuscript, fixing his eyes upon his guest, trying to determine whether the somewhat height-challenged individual was seated or standing. "Very pleased to meet you," he said, reaching across his desk, inviting a handshake. Instead of taking the extended hand, the visiting scientist crouched and began peering up into the editor's face.

Startled, the editor stooped in an effort to meet his guest eye to eye. This caused the doctor to drop to his knees, which triggered Mr. Duster to lie flat on his desk, which caused the ornithologist to go down on all fours. His concentration on the editor's face never wavered.

"Your nostrils are vunderful," he exclaimed.

"Thank you," the editor exclaimed. "Yours are nice too," he added (although, in truth, he had yet to see the dorsal side of the man's nose). "You study human nostrils as well as bird nostrils?" he assessed, juxtaposing the man's antics and subject of his book proposal—*A Field Guide to Avian Nasal Mites.*

"Nein," he said, drawing a magnifying glass from a jacket pocket, peering intently into the editor's left nostril. "Der nostril ist just der environment. It ist der mites dat I study."

"Of course," Mr. Duster said, drawing away, raising the book proposal between them in a successful bid to prevent the doctor from pursuing him across the desk. "And your premise is that all birds can be differentiated on the basis of nasal mites that are specific to that bird species?"

"Der ist no question," the scientist replied. "Every bird on der planet can be identified by der mites alone even better den der DNA."

"Fascinating," the editor exclaimed, considering the possibilities, growing excited about scooping the entire field guide industry. "So by using your system even look-alike species can be identified in the field?"

"Ya. Mit my field guide to der nasal mites, even der *Empidonax* flycatchers are as plain now as der nose on der face. Here, I show you," he said, taking the manuscript, flipping to a series of magnified photos showing creatures so ugly that they would induce sleeplessness in Steven King.

"Dis ist der mite from der least flycatcher. See how it ist small und gray mit a round head und stubby mandibles. Now der acadian flycatcher mite. See. Bigger und on der back greener, ya?"

"I, uh, well, I guess," the editor replied, "but . . ."

"A bad photo," the doctor explained. "An adult mite dat ist very worn. In der book, we use a better photo, ya?"

"Also," he said, "der habitat ist different. Der least mite ist always at der edge of der thick, hairy growth und only near to der wet places. Der acadian mite ist always where der hair ist thickest und der nostril wettest."

"Do they vocalize?" the editor wanted to know.

"Ya, der least mite says 'ah-CHOO,' der acadian mite 'AH-choo.' Ist very different."

"I see," said the editor. "How about western and cordilleran flycatchers?"

"Ah," the doctor said, warming to the subject. "Here," he said, flipping to the next page.

"I don't see any difference," the editor confessed.

"Der ist no difference," the scientist exclaimed triumphantly. "But der western flycatcher mite ist always found in der right bird nostril. Der cordilleran in der left."

"This is fantastic," the editor exclaimed. "This could revolutionize bird identification."

"Und der scientific study too. Here, der green heron." The scientist flipped to another page, one showing two ugly-looking creatures—one dark and labeled "Striated," the other pale and labeled "Green-Backed."

"These are *very* different," the editor exclaimed. "Clearly different species."

"Nein, nein, nein," the Doctor stuttered. "Der mites are der same just as der birds are der same. Only der views are different. In der North America bird der mites on der tummy lie. In der South America, always on der back."

"Remarkable," the editor exclaimed. "The only question I have is, how do you see the mites in the field?"

"Ah," the doctor exclaimed, winking. "Dat ist der trick, ya? You use der salt solution."

The editor didn't say anything for a moment. Then it occurred to him that perhaps the doctor was making a joke.

"You mean you have to be very close—close enough to put salt on its tail?"

"Nein," the Doctor explained. "You must squirt der saline solution into der bird's nostril und take a sample to study through der microscope. Ist only way."

"I see," the editor said.

"Vat I offer you ist right of first refusal," the doctor said, beaming.

"Exactly right," the editor replied.

Part 5

REFLECTIONS

THE FOX AND THE HARRIER

The harrier, an adult male, was sitting in the open marsh, half-hidden in grass. The bird was calm, nominally alert, but perhaps a little too preoccupied with its preening. This is how the fox managed to get so close.

The animal was stalking the harrier from behind, using the grassy lip of a tidal creek to best strategic advantage. From where the harrier sat, the fox was invisible. From my position I could see it all, and from my estimates I could envision only one outcome to the unfolding drama.

What should I do? I like foxes—because they are beautiful and intelligent, and because they are marvelously skilled predators. But I like harriers too, and for the very same reasons. In fact, among all of New Jersey's nesting birds, the northern harrier is my clear favorite.

The choices were these: I could interfere, cheat the fox out of its meal but save the harrier; or I could do nothing, gaining insight perhaps but at the expense of a favorite creature's demise. It was a dilemma.

This is going to be an odd essay, and maybe a boring essay, and maybe an irritating essay as well. But it is an essay I have a mind to write and the point it raises is one worth taking to heart. Its philosophical roots are buried in a life of wildlife observation, but its impetus was prompted by the juxtaposition of several disparate events.

These events linked up and framed an answer to an age-old question, one I now pose to you: What is our role in nature?

No, no, you can't take the high road, assume that lofty heroic stand that humanity has no role in nature. It's too late for the creature that fished out the Grand Banks, lubricated Prince William Sound, and blew a frog-scorching hole in the ozone layer to play Pontius Pilate.

As a member of the species that is usurping the planet and monopolizing its resources, I believe that it is our responsibility to know when to step in and intercede, or intrude, when nature gets into a bind. Thanks to the fox and harrier, the members of the North American Rehabilitators Association, and Tom, I think I've found an answer.

Tom is a hunter, an environmentalist, and a writer for one of the Big Three hook and bullet magazines. Tom was doing a column on hunters who are also environmentalists; he wanted my input and the subject of management came up. Many hunters consider conservation and management to be synonymous, but they are not.

Conservation is an ethic that opposes destruction, misuse, or erosion of natural resources. It is nonspecific and its essence is restraint.

Management is the manipulation of habitat and animals to benefit one species or group of species over others. It is a tool. It is specific. And its essence is action.

Conservation the ethic and management the tool both involve conscious choices with regard to the environment. The conservation movement started in the last century when overhunting and habitat destruction reduced much of North America's wildlife to a vestige of its former abundance. The solution was restraint *and* management—and it worked! Much of North America's depleted wildlife was restored.

In this century, management has been used primarily to keep the populations of assorted wildlife populations—principally game species—high. But management is selective. It benefits species that humans assign value. And while it is often tangentially beneficial to other, nontarget species, it may be and usually is detrimental to others.

Take the American woodcock, an upland shorebird and a popular gamebird. Woodcock numbers have been declining. Why? Because woodcock require open fields and new growth woodlands ("edge"). As forests in the Northeast have matured in the last half of this century, woodcock habitat has decreased.

The response of game management engineers has been to encourage landowners and refuge managers to cut swaths through mature woodlands, creating edge. Now here's the rub: creating edge benefits the woodcock, but it is detrimental to many species of woodland songbird. Edge is an open door for cowbirds, and cowbirds parasitize songbird nests, resulting in reduced nest productivity. Both woodcock and songbirds are declining, and the management policy is tantamount to stealing from Peter (and John and Matthew and Simon . . .) to give to Paul.

At least that's how I read it. At least this is the sort of institutionalized interference that led me to conclude, long ago, that too often wildlife management is biased manipulation predicated upon human interest, not natural diversity and broad-scope biological need.

And this is what early on in my writing career led me to profess that the best way to maintain an environment is to just plain leave it alone. Don't interfere. Don't manage. Just let nature strike her own, proper balance.

If anything should be managed, it's people, not wildlife.

This laissez-faire conclusion led to a hard-line conviction. When people called my office and said, "I've got this bird that has fallen out of the nest. What should I do?" I said, "Put it back." When someone tells me woodcock are declining because forests are maturing, I say, "Sounds natural enough to me."

Then, right after my conversation with Tom, while this management question was still fresh in my mind, I attended the Wildlife Rehabilitators annual meeting. It served to undermine my laissez-faire stance.

Good folks, these rehab people. As concerned about stressed and injured wildlife as the founders of the conservation movement were concerned about the wildlife heritage of a continent.

Wildlife rehab people are the ones that get to go one-on-one with preschoolers with twenty grams of baby robin clutched in their hands and tears down both cheeks. Wildlife rehab people are the ones conservation officers turn to when the peregrine falcon is found in the marsh with a wing half torn off by shot—because some fool can't tell the difference between a falcon and a duck, or because some brigand disguised as a hunter puts his perverted vanity above the law of the land.

And wildlife rehab people are the ones that get called in when vessels rupture and oil casts trouble upon the waters, causing death and injury to hundreds and thousands of birds and animals. Rehab people use their skills and they direct resources to salvage what can be salvaged and redress a wrong committed against nature. They *interfere* because a wrong has been done, and it is up to responsible people to set it right.

Just as those founders of conservation once did.

So I came to modify my position about management. I'm still very much of the opinion that an environment is maintained best when it is juggled least. I am still of the opinion that it's people who need management, not wildlife.

But since our species cannot be part of this world and not part of the environment—since our encroachments are bound to have impacts and these will have to be redressed—then this is how I view humanity's role in nature.

As the custodians of the planet, we are obligated to restore nature when some action of ours threatens or degrades it. But as creatures who are not all-knowing and cannot foresee all ends, we are wise to let nature establish her own order and limits without imposing preferences or biases.

I decided to do nothing. I decided not to warn the harrier or deflect the fox, and although I did not *like* my decision I was comfortable with it.

The fox crept near. The harrier suspected nothing. And just as the fox paused, gathering itself for its leap, the harrier calmly stretched, muted, and flew, leaving a naturally foiled fox and a vindicated observer behind.

VESPERS FOR A FALLOUT

When I was little, all the neighborhood kids used to sit on our front steps and listen for the two sounds that would spark a summer evening. The first was the jingle of the ice-cream truck; the second was the sputter of the DDT fogger.

The ice-cream truck usually arrived first, and we'd fight for the privilege of squandering our allowances on smoking Popsicles and vanilla ice cream covered in dye-colored grit. The fogger usually arrived just before dark, just before the wood thrush, singing vespers, retired for the night. Popsicles in hand, we'd chase the fogger down the street, running in and out of the chemical cloud, laughing all the way.

It was harmless, after all. The grownups told us this; the government too! And we were children. We were obedient. And we had never been betrayed. We accepted the wisdom of grownups and governments on faith.

"There. Above the trees," wife Linda directed, bringing her Bausch and Lomb 8×42s to bear. We saw them immediately, a weary string of birds holding just above the trees.

"Or-i-oles," Judy Toups pronounced, studying the slim icterid lines, dragging out the syllables the way folks who live in Mississippi do.

"Orchard [orioles]," I added, noting the burnt orange plumage ignited by a rising sun.

"And a northern," Linda amended, picking the trailing odd-bird-out of the flock.

"GoOod," Judy intoned, assessing both Linda's skills and our fortune. As local expert and our guide, this was Judy's prerogative and privilege.

Behind the first group of birds was another, this one comprised of rose-breasted grosbeaks, wings flashing silver dollar–sized patches of white. Mixed in were scarlet tanagers, unmistakable at any distance. A wave of eastern kingbirds followed, blunt-headed birds whose fluttery wingbeat makes them look like they are perpetually trying to catch up.

Then another flock of orioles (sprinkled with tanagers).

Then tanagers sprinkled with orioles. Another.

Another.

More kingbirds.

More orioles.

Spring fallout on the Mississippi Coast.

We'd been birding the Gulf Coast for a week, hoping, praying for the great precipitation of wings that birders dream of. Praying for a second chance.

"You should have been here Thursday," Judy had announced upon our Saturday arrival. "ThOUSAnds of birds," she pronounced, letting the syllables climb in measure with the flight. "Thousands," she repeated, expressing both the wonder and injustice of it all.

"What's the weather picture look like for the rest of the week?" I asked, trying not to sound too hopeful (and fooling no one, least of all Judy).

"There's *supposed* to be another cold front coming through," Judy guardedly advised. "But not until later in the week. We'll keep an eye on the weather maps and play it by ear."

Front or no front, there would still be birds to enjoy, of course. Resident species like Swainson's warbler and swallow-tailed kites—birds that a couple of vagabond birders from New Jersey would be thrilled to see. And there would be migrants too. Birds traveling northbound on the Yucatán Express—the

cuckoos, flycatchers, thrushes, vireos, warblers, tanagers, grosbeaks, and orioles—that vault the Gulf of Mexico every spring.
But without a cold front and its daunting wall of rain, the mass of
migrating birds would overshoot the coast and forage inland.

This is why, every spring, birders from Texas to the Tortugas
head for the Gulf Coast, watch the weather maps, and pray for rain.

We prayed too and watched as the jagged-toothed line marked
with a capital *H* marched down from Canada on the Sunday
evening news. We cheered as the advancing line cleared the Dako-
tas on Monday and held our breath as it plunged into neighboring
Arkansas on Tuesday.

But by Wednesday the front had crept no closer than northern
Mississippi. The system was losing steam, and a typically diffi-
dent weather forecaster changed his earlier prediction from "rain
Thursday," to "chance of showers in the northern part of the
state." It sure sounded as though the system was going to stall.

Judy, hoping to flaunt the strategic riches of Mississippi, was
vexed. Linda and I were bummed.

Sure enough, Thursday dawned uneventfully sunny or, as Judy
put it, "There is nothing more boring than a blue sky." We skipped
the news that night, opting instead to eat out at a neat little hole-
in-the-wall ribs place, smothering our disappointment with barbe-
cue sauce and a few beers.

On the way home, it started to sprinkle. Then it started to rain.
Then it started to *pour*—poured so hard, in fact, that the wind-
shield wipers bowed under the strain. Poured so hard that by the
time we got back to our room, we didn't park the car so much as
dock it.

The storms continued off and on all night, filling our room with
lightning flashes and our dreams with sweet anticipation. Just offshore, over the stormy Gulf of Mexico, a drama was unfolding.
Beneath a dark, directionless sky, weary birds were fighting for
their lives and many were losing.

The story of the great masses of migrating birds that carpet the
Gulf Coast has a tragic side, a dark irony that taints every fall-

out. The conditions that produce masses of birds for birders bring despair for the birds themselves. When the great storms lash out across the Gulf of Mexico, birds die. The coastal fallouts that birders dream of are comprised of weary survivors.

In the weeks before their cross-gulf journey, migrating songbirds prepare by feeding voraciously, putting on fat, the fuel that they will consume during their flight. Cargo restrictions are severe for birds whose weight is measured in grams. Fully loaded, a hooded warbler may top out at thirteen grams, one-third of which is fuel. It is enough to see them across the Gulf under normal, favorable conditions. But there is little excess to spare.

Every evening, from late March until early May, North America's long-distance migrants initiate their great leaps of faith. Despite the hardship and the risk, bird migration is a strategy for survival. It permits many kinds of birds to distribute themselves across northern reaches of the planet at a time when winter's retreat creates an abundance of food and space. Then, when winter begins closing its fist over the land, migration offers birds a means of escape.

Without migration, many of North America's nesting birds would never have extended their ranges northward. Without migration, the number and diversity of birds seen in North America on June 1 would differ little from what might be seen on January 1.

Leveling out at two to four thousand feet, the migrating birds travel all night, navigating, like all great voyagers, by the stars. If their fortune holds, they will reach the United States mainland. There they will seek out the habitat that meets their peculiar needs to rest and feed.

But often things do not go well. As all great voyagers know, great gains are bought at great risk. Cold fronts pushing offshore greet birds with a wall of clouds. Rain drags at their wings. Head winds slow their progress, adding hours to the flight, wasting fuel.

When the last of their fat reserve is spent, as the birds begin to metabolize the muscle tissue that holds them aloft, they weaken and lose altitude. Soon only desperation keeps them above the reach of the waves.

For thirty minutes, we watched as flock after straggling flock labored across the woodland clearing, putting distance between themselves and the Gulf of Mexico. The terrible night was over; the aquatic hurdle vaulted.

"Let's get over to Ansley," Judy coached. "If it's good here, it will be *great* over there." Ansley is a chenier (pronounced shin-ear)—a wooded hummock surrounded by open marsh, a migrant trap of the first magnitude.

We parked right on the road (inconveniencing no one). Without hesitation (or insect repellent), we entered the finger of trees reaching out into open marsh, and what we discovered was a surprise but hardly a disappointment. Yes, there were grosbeaks (and tanagers and orioles) at Ansley, but not in the saturation numbers we'd expected. The treasure of Ansley was measured in the number of thrushes seeking sanctuary beneath the trees. Dozens of thrushes. Scores! The woodland was alive with these denizens of the forest floor.

Prominent in the ranks were burly wood thrushes—the bird whose evening song was as much a part of summer as Popsicles and pop flies. Also racing beneath the chenier were other thrushes, slighter and slimmer, and veery, darker and secretive, and Swainson's.

The game in Mississippi (and in many other places) is to pan through the Swainson's thrushes and find the gremlin gray-cheeked, a thrush disguised as a shadow. Birding is not a spectator sport, thank God. If it was, we would have drawn the laughter of the gallery by trying to sneak up on birds whose evasive skills border on artistry. Every bird we approached responded by stalking directly away, avoiding sunlight with a finesse that would make any vampire proud to be an understudy. Coincidentally, running interference for the birds was a host of winged vampires—mosquitoes—who quickly ascertained that birders in pursuit of a possible gray-cheeked thrush are an easy mark.

By the time the game was over, the chenier covered end to end, we had collectively banked what even the stingiest among us would call 2½ countable gray-cheeks, approximately seventy veerys, as many wood thrushes, and two dozen Swainson's—more thrushes than I had ever seen in one place at one time. But the real winners in the event were the mosquitoes, who drew first blood and last and may have collectively banked as much as a quart and a half.

We didn't grudge the loss of vital fluids. Mosquitoes come with the turf, are part of a functioning, natural environment. Take away the mosquitoes, take away the insects, and starving birds have no recourse but to starve. A corner of the world as globally significant to migrating birds as the Mississippi Coast is worth a few mosquito bites.

We had almost reached Judy's car before we heard the sound of an approaching vehicle—a truck of some sort; a truck that sounded like it was running on about half its cylinders.

It was a sound that was vaguely familiar. A sound linked to memories of Popsicles and pop flies. But before memory could index it, the truck came into view—a country mosquito truck spraying the chenier with a chemical mist, killing insects in a strip of woods that serves only to house mosquitoes and preserve the lives of migrating birds.

For just a moment, I thought I heard, once again, the song of the wood thrush singing vespers in my parents' backyard. But it's certain I was mistaken. It's been many years of attrition since wood thrushes sang there. And the birds foraging in Ansley, on the coast of Mississippi, were too weary and too hungry for song.

AFTER THE COLD FRONT

After the cold front went through, the clouds were driven back and the stars crept out of hiding. The hosts of purple martins rose before the dawn and greeted the stars with the chuckles and scolding chortles of their ink-colored kind.

They would spend much of the day aloft, these largest of North America's swallows. They would soar on swept-back wings, feast upon the transient, spot-winged glider dragonflies who hitch their fortunes to the wind and use it to transport themselves hundreds of miles. In the afternoon, the martins would descend and sheath the utility wires in the town. Visitors walking the streets would wonder at the great numbers of swallows and marvel that any place could be so blessed.

After the cold front went through, the warblers, which had waited so long for the proper conditions, were carried far from breeding territories in the north. Some were older adult birds, but most were juveniles, apprentices making the South American run for the first time. At dawn, over the waters that surround the tip of the Cape May peninsula, they began to descend, seeking shelter for the day.

They passed over the heads of surf fishermen, joggers, and early morning strollers. They buried themselves in the hedges and woodlots and shrub-strewn meadows. It was early in the season and the morning free of hawks, so they fed in the open, moving like multicolored sparks among the leaves, darting out now and again to snatch some moth who mistakenly believed that there was safety in flight.

The fishermen, who cast their lines and their sights out to sea, were surprised to find so many small birds coming in off the water. They looked so fragile and so tired, and when the gulls closed in and snapped up many in their bills, they felt bad for the birds— or would have, except that the bluefish began a blitz; rods began to bend, and catching fish became more important than feeling sorry for birds.

After the cold front went through, the massed flocks of terns grew restless and flighty because they knew the day of departure was at hand. For weeks they had gathered on the beaches in harsh-voiced clusters—gray-backed adults and scallop-backed birds of the year. On the ground, they waddled more than walked and took flight only to feed and to avoid the charge of unleashed dogs.

Flushed, they rose like angry smoke, cursing the dog and its owner in the language of terns. Eventually they would settle or, turning the disruption to utilitarian use, would go offshore to feed. Just beyond the breakers or on the horizon far offshore, they would hover in killing clouds over the schools of baitfish that the bluefish massacred from below.

Among the flocks were diminutive least terns with petite yellow bills and larger common terns with bills the color of arterial blood. They sliced into the water, plucking small silver-sided fish from innocence, then hurried toward shore before the brigand gulls could catch them.

After the cold front went through, large numbers of monarch butterflies began moving down the beach, hugging the dunes, flying with stiff-winged determination. There were scores of the insects in view and, by simple extrapolation, thousands cleaving a path down the Cape May peninsula. The insects were engaged in the first leg of their relay race to Mexico. The first winds of autumn had given them both urgency and speed.

In the evening, when the wind stilled and cold air enfolded land, the monarchs sought shelter on the sunny side of wind-sculpted cedar trees. Wings closed, the insects appear to be nothing more than dead leaves. In this way they defeated all but the eyes of the sharpest onlookers. In this way they found passage through the night.

After the cold front went through, the hummingbirds that had been moving in small numbers since early August picked up the tempo of migration. At the observation platform at Cape May Point State Park, the lilliputian forms were zipping over the heads of onlookers at five-to-ten-minute intervals. In the evening, when the tiny wings wearied, townspeople who put up hummingbird feeders would be treated to a host of hungry birds. Along woodland edges, where the orange-blossomed trumpet vines flourished, the vagrants would compete with resident hummingbirds for nectar.

Cold makes hummingbirds hungry. The energetic demands of migration make them hungry too—hungry and incautious. Along a bushy edge, a young hummingbird drawn to a surfeit of flowers, blundered into the web of a large black-and-yellow garden spider. Its struggles brought the web's owner and, in time, exhaustion.

Hungry is as hungry does, and nature does not discriminate.

After the cold front went through, the first of the American kestrels began to move. Brown-backed females and harlequin-colored males, the small falcons swept over the dunes and along the water's edge in groups of three, four, and five, rising and falling like knotted streamers in the wind.

They appeared in pulses that quickened as the afternoon wore on. Each new group was greeted with enthusiasm by those assembled on the observation platform, until a shout brought all heads up. In moments, all optics were focused upon the large plank-winged raptor soaring overhead.

It didn't have a white head and it didn't have a white tail, but it was nonetheless a bald eagle. The kestrels and the eagles were the vanguard of what is one of the greatest concentrations of migrating birds of prey in North America. From mid-August until the end of November, it would be a rare moment when some bird of prey would not be visible over the platform—conditions permitting, of course (which is very much the point of this essay, in case you have not guessed).

After the cold front went through, sweeping summer before it and ushering a taste of autumn in behind, it kept on moving, traveling farther offshore. The winds that circle in a clockwise pattern around high-pressure centers went from northwest to northerly to northeasterly and then they slackened. As the center of the high passed, the winds turned southerly, pumping warm, moist air back into the region and bringing a return to summer.

Two days after the cold front went through, the people in the towns walked beneath empty utility wires, and the green-head flies that hatched after the purple martins left made life miserable for those wearing shorts.

The morning sky was empty of warblers; the beaches devoid of terns. Migrating monarch butterflies were only a vestige of their cold front–spurred numbers, and hummingbirds were hardly to be found except on the shady side of gardens, where summer lingered.

On the platform at Cape May Point State Park, those savvy watchers who knew the cause and effect relation between weather and wildlife were nowhere to be seen. They would return when the next cold front arrived. In fact, the only people around were casual visitors, who climbed the stairs lured by the optimistic promise of the sign that read Official Hawk Watch.

They'd stay a minute or two. Put a quarter in the pay-per-view optics and scan the horizon. Then, finding nothing to entertain them, they'd leave—wondering what perversity would prompt the state to establish a natural area in a place that clearly didn't have any wildlife.

BONDED TO THE WEST WIND

I am bonded to the West Wind—and its ally the North Wind (and the East and South Winds, and all the hybrid winds that lie between). But mostly I follow the West Wind. When the axis of the earth inclines toward autumn, I follow it to mountain peaks and peninsula points as surely as migrating birds are driven before it.

In July and August, the West Wind ferries shorebirds my way. Dowitchers and yellowlegs, plovers and peep—fresh from the Arctic tundra, deposited daily on tidal flats and reservoir shores. For weeks on end, mud and mud-colored birds are the focus of my life. Even my name (when I arrive two hours late for work) is Mudd.

Then it's September and my windy liege shakes down the branches of northern forests, sending a storm of passerines my way. Warblers that move like multicolored sparks, thrushes that cloak themselves in shadows by day and whose nocturnal passage is heralded by a nasal yelp in the night.

But October and November are the months when the West Wind really shows its stuff. That is when the wind masters themselves, the birds of prey, surf its currents south. Important tasks turn to trifles when buteos mount the skies and falcons cruise the coast. If there is a sight to surpass an eagle pinned to a ridge, I've never dreamed it. (And if anyone has ever run a correlation between northwest winds and worker absenteeism, I'll bet its pretty direct.)

Worshiping the West Wind has a price. Every morning before dawn, my faith obligates me to sit in front of the TV and tune in to that great oracle of our time: the weather channel. Coffee in hand, eyes fused to the screen, I study the meteorological battle lines and pray.

If things auger well (i.e., if the front has cleared), one sitting through the local forecast is all that faith asks. But if the meteorological priests warn of a stalled front or raise the specter of a series of lows forming along the frontal boundary, I'll sit through coffee cup after cup, watching the local radar, trying to boost the barometric reading with longing and hope.

Wife Linda says I'm addicted. She claims she can't understand how a grown man can sit (within twenty feet of a sink full of dishes) and stare at simulated thundershowers crawling across a TV screen at ten-minute intervals. She doesn't comprehend how a front stalled over the Great Lakes or wind a few degrees east of north can make all the life-and-death difference in the world.

Actually she does understand. She just refuses to admit it while there are dishes in the sink.

If washing dishes could jump-start a stalled front, I'd be up to my elbows in suds. If wearing a lucky charm could affect the weather, I'd dress like a Christmas tree.

But I am charmed by the wind, not the charmer. I go where it goes, when it directs me. To pinnacles and peninsula points. Where I stand with other followers amid the wind-driven stream of birds, grateful for whatever fortune the West Wind blows my way.

MY PERFECT UNIVERSE

The wind almost took the car door out of my hands, would have if I hadn't been prepared for it. It cut like a cold-edged file and flayed exposed portions of my anatomy—not that there were many.

"Thank heavens I don't have to live out here," I thought. "There couldn't be any survivors," I added.

With this heavy thought to motivate me, I started for the meadows. Despite the cold, despite my certainty, I still hoped fervently to find at least one of the flock of tree swallows still alive.

There had been forty or so tree swallows at Cape May Point before temperatures took the plunge. They'd been here all winter, fortunate beneficiaries of an uncommonly warm season. Most of these emerald-backed insect-eating birds don't linger farther north than the outer banks of North Carolina. Along the Gulf Coast, where winters are mild, they accumulate in hordes.

But like many creatures, the winter's mild temperatures had seduced them. Why, in Cape May there were even butterfly sightings in mid-January: an orange sulphur and a mourning cloak!

Then the jet stream took a dive. Then things began to die.

The day after the temperatures dropped into the single digits, the number of tree swallows had been halved. Yesterday, three days after the cold front hit town, the numbers were halved again.

The frayed flock sat on the ice for the most part. Sometimes they would take wing and flutter like candle flames in the wind. Then they would settle. It was clear they were starving. It was futile to try to save them. And they were just the visible tip of the iceberg. All around me in the frozen marsh, there were creatures succumbing to the killing cold—rails, bitterns, herons, even some hardy ducks and geese. It tried my humanity. It called my truce with the universe into question—a question I thought I had resolved long ago.

When I was younger, I was very much interested in understanding why nature was as it was. In particular, I wanted to know why it was that nature was a regular killing field. I wanted an accounting for why life was bounded by so much pain and death.

I'm not saying there isn't a dark, beautiful symmetry to it. Things live, things die, pain is the usher. I'm just saying why not . . . not death, just life?

It seemed a defensible alternative. And since I was young, and since I could not find a comparable solution among the answers handed down by the adults, I decided to do the universe over and this time do it right.

Not being as gifted at creating as the Creator, I found rather quickly that I could not envision a completely different universe than the one I was in. So I was forced to fall back on a plan that emphasized "new and improved" as opposed to "completely different."

I decided to take the universe as we know it and just start working backward. You know. Like a new manager coming into a botched operation. I'd assess the situation, salvage what I could, and do away with all the things that were bad.

The first thing I decided to do away with in this bold new universe was predators—those creatures that survive by killing other things. Nasty business, predation. Very hurtful.

There would be no more lions or tigers or polar bears in this perfect world I was creating. No killer whales or sharks or rattlesnakes.

Or hawks or owls (even though I really liked hawks and owls). Or worm-killing robins or insect-eating swallows. Or bats or krill-filtering whales or ladybugs or lap cats—at least lap cats that killed birds at feeders. No killers. That was the rule.

It would certainly mean a less diverse world. But if it meant a safer world—one in which no creature caused pain or death to another—it was worth it.

Then I concluded I'd have to do something about winter. Winter, after all, killed things too. Crickets that made music and butterflies that made gardens animate; fireflies that made nights come alive and sparrows who froze to their perches when the chilling winds crept out of the north.

It was settled. No winter. I righted the tilt in the earth's axis, fixing permanently the apportionment of warmth over the face of the planet. It meant, of course, that life couldn't distribute itself as far as it did under the old system when seasons moved across the earth. There could never be life at the poles, and everything would be more or less crowded around the planet's middle, but . . .

But that was certainly a small price to pay for a perfect world, particularly since we'd gotten rid of all the predators and had a lot more room than we used to have. We'd all be one big, happy family living in the fat middle of an agrarian planet.

Then it occurred to me that even plants have a right to exist. What if they had feelings and just couldn't express them? What if they felt pain and were as desperate to live as everything else? And even if they weren't conscious, they were, as living things, privileged. They had as much right to live as anything else.

So in my perfect world I decided to do away with the herbivores too. Anything that nibbled leaves or bored holes in stems or gnawed seeds—terminated. Out of here.

That really narrowed down the players in my perfect world. In fact, it seemed that I was left with a wonderful bunch of nectar-feeding creatures—hummingbirds, butterflies, and honeybees.

Then it occurred to me that there wasn't any need for flowers. Because in a perfect world in which nothing died there was no reason to procreate. Have a lot of unchecked procreation in a perfect world and pretty soon you have overcrowding—which is less than perfect.

So I did away with procreation. If nothing dies, nothing needs replacement, right?

Now I really had a lot of room. In fact, my perfect world seemed to exist solely for creatures that were able to convert sunlight into food—the process called photosynthesis. Plants can do this . . . and a few microscopic organisms too.

I'd just learned about photosynthesis in biology. We'd done experiments involving microorganisms too. Then I recalled one experiment where we had subjected a bunch of microscopic organisms to light. And how they had tried to get away from the light, seeking the shelter of some shadow.

We didn't call it light, of course. We called it a negative stimulus, but the result was the same. The critters skedaddled like they'd been burned.

So in my perfect world—my hurtless, harmless world—there could be no light, I decided. It would be like the womb. It would be like the universe before hurt. It would be perfect. And so I said the words.

"Let there be darkness." And in my mind, it was so.

It didn't take long before I started adding elements of imperfection back into my perfect universe. Perfection might be perfect, but it is also boring. And life might be painful, but take it from me, it sure seems better than perfection.

There might be other ways to put a universe together—one in which tree swallows do not die; one in which life exists without risk. But after having taken creation back to the big bang and having taken upon myself the grave privilege of putting my finger in the dike to save a priceless nothing, I have chosen instead to accept life's pattern as it has evolved and hope, even if I sometimes find it hard to believe, that there is reason.

I navigated the meadows quickly because it was cold. It was empty—at least it was empty of tree swallows. During the night, huddled together in the *Phragmites,* the last of them had died.

I hope it didn't hurt them too much. I hope that there is a reason. But even if there is no reason, there is life, which I accept as the foundation of my faith. Risk may be the price, and the price is high, but the alternative? The alternative is hollow.

SPRING OF WONDER,
AUTUMN OF MASTERY

It seems to me (with apologies extended to Hermann Hesse) that human lives are trapped between opposing poles. We aspire to freedom but crave security. We work toward what is right and good, but our feet invariably wander off the path of righteousness and into the tangles.

My regard for birds has been this way too: two-sided. On the one hand, the appeal of birds is aesthetic and emotional. It puts the "Wow!" in cardinals and the "Isn't that sweet?" in a chick-a-dee-dee-dee. The other side of my focus is acquisitive and analytical. It imparts significance to things like anchor-shaped patterns on scapulars, and it prompts me to stand in 103-degree heat in search of some bird whose only real appeal is that I have never seen it before.

Aesthetic appeal and analytical/acquisitive interest—the twin poles of birding. In my life they are represented by two experiences. The first I dubbed the Spring of Discovery; the second, the Autumn of Mastery. Neither event, I am inclined to believe, could be replicated today.

The Spring of Discovery occurred in May 1962. I was eleven and enjoying ill health (which means I was *supposed* to be quietly convalescing from minor surgery but wasn't). Instead, I was busy running around my parents' backyard trying to gain fragmentary glimpses of tiny treetop birds.

My parents' backyard was pretty typical of Suburbia, U.S.A.—
a postage-stamp patch of grass ringed by trees. I'd started watching birds at the age of seven, and I'd seen a lot of good birds in
that yard. Blue jays of the brassy voices, nesting brown thrasher
that go right for your nose, tufted titmice . . . white-breasted nuthatches . . . and a tidy swarm of robin nestlings whose forsaken
lives begged saving. Oh, I was one hotshot backyard birder all
right. The best in the neighborhood.

But whatever my assumed proficiency, I had no sense of migration, no grasp of the biannual drama that carries discovery to every
suburban doorstep. That all changed in 1962. That's what the
Spring of Discovery was all about.

I guess I conned Mom into letting me sit outside. I guess I must
have gotten bored with whatever school assignments I'd been
saddled with and looked up at the tops of the oaks, and seen all
the activity up there.

I guess I must have sprin . . . that is, limped painfully . . . into
the house. And got my father's 6×24 binoculars. And the National
Geographic Society's book about song and garden birds that
served as my field guide.

I can stop guessing from this point. I *know* what happened
next. My eyes grew wide with discovery and a host of images
poured in. Thirty-five years later I can still recall each vivid encounter.

There was the zebra-striped warbler that moved like a nuthatch
and the white-bottomed one whose back—when you finally got to
see the back—was the even color of cool, green jade. There were
yellow-bellied ones with necklaces and yellow-bellied ones without necklaces—and there was one, one absolutely, unbelievably
beautiful-beyond-expression *one* whose throat was the color of a
flame trapped in amber.

That one was called the Blackburnian. That one was my
favorite.

There were other birds too. Baltimore orioles that glowed like
peeled orange crayons, scarlet tanagers that blazed within their
leafy confines like fanned charcoal in a patio grill. There was also

one beautiful black-and-white bird whose bill was chalky white and whose chest bore a crimson bib.

That one was the rose-breasted grosbeak. That one was my favorite too.

It is interesting to note that bird song played no part in the Spring of Discovery, although certainly birds were just as vocal in 1962 as they are today. I wasn't interested in song. I was captivated by color.

It is also interesting to note that the flood of birds was not fallout-dependent (as migration in the Northeast is today). The day-to-day number and diversity were as constant as a shifting kaleidoscope. Morning or afternoon, I could pass my eyes through the treetops and relish the feeling of wonder. And I did too.

That was the Spring of Discovery. It spanned two weeks and lasted a lifetime. There have been many wonderful moments of discovery since then, but no time when wonder has so dominated the world.

The Autumn of Mastery came a little over a decade later. I was just out of college, jobbing as a carpet installer, and I had once again discovered the lure of birds. But something in my regard was different. Something had changed. I wasn't merely interested in seeing birds and enjoying birds—not exactly. What I was really interested in was seeking out birds that I had never seen before and pinning names to them.

I was also frustrated and angry. Frustrated because the plumages of the "confusing fall warblers" were all so *confusing*. Angry because my marginal field identification skills were holding me back, preventing me from seeing the subtle distinctions that would add species to my list.

So one day in early September, on a morning so cool it brought a jacket out of the closet, I grabbed my binoculars and went into the woods—to a brushy clearing surrounded by second-growth forest that bordered a lake. I staked myself out in the center of the clearing vowing to "learn 'em or die." The outcome, for the first hour or so, was never certain.

All around the clearing, little green birds flickered and danced.

Dozens of them. Scores! They almost never sat in the open. They never took perches for long. And every time my binoculars were brought to bear some sixth sense seemed to warn them that their identities were in jeopardy. They reacted by boring little warbler-sized holes into the foliage.

As minutes passed and my angst mounted, the "confusing fall warblers" became those "frustrating fall warblers," became those "damned fall warblers." But just when my pique was reaching its peak, my binoculars chanced to fall upon one particular yellow-bellied bird—and the kaleidoscope stopped shifting.

In many respects, it was like all the rest of the birds in the clearing. Just another green and yellow bird with wing bars and white in the tail. But there was something different about its chest. The chest had a pale gray band across it, like the critter had been tie-dyed or something.

The band wasn't as sharply defined as wing bars and tail spots—those little building blocks of identification that I had dutifully learned and had come to count on. It was subtle, the mere shadow of a field mark. But it was nevertheless discernable, and it differentiated the bird from all the rest. The question was, *was* it a field mark?

I looked at the plate in the book. And there it was. The telltale mark. The tie-dyed warbler. An immature magnolia.

"*Gotcha,*" I whispered, and it came out a hiss. "Got you." And that's all it took. One catalytic bird. One bird to serve as a measure of comparison for all the rest. Gradually, one by cryptic one, the other denizens of the glen surrendered their identities—chestnut-sided warblers (without chestnut sides), yellow warblers (that weren't yellow), bay-breasted warblers (sans bay). One by one, I gathered them with my growing arsenal of skills.

There is something interesting about the phrase "got you." It denotes possession, and possession is a form of control. I didn't consciously realize this at the time. It wasn't, in fact, until years later that I was able to put the acquisitive side of birding into perspective. The catalyst was a work of fantasy written by Ursula Le Guin called *Earthsea Trilogy.* In this trilogy, Le Guin describes an elemental language, the language of the Beginning. In this language, all things are known by their true names. The language is secret, of course—known only to dragons and the odd wizard or two—and this is good. Why? Because anyone who knows the language and the true name of a thing has mastery over that thing. They control it.

That's what I was doing during the Autumn of Mastery. I was pinning names to birds and making them mine. For most of my adult birding life, my focus has been the naming and claiming of birds . . . and the acquisition of greater skills to apply to these ambitions.

The Spring of Discovery and the Autumn of Mastery—pivotal events that anchored my perspective and my life. Maybe other birders know a similar development; maybe not. But one thing I do know. Were I growing up in Whippany, New Jersey, today, it is unlikely that I would have the benefit of those experiences to anchor the poles of my life.

Why? Because now in spring there is no river of birds sweeping through the trees around my parents' house. There is not even a steady stream. What passes in May is hardly a trickle. The swarm of treetop birds who snared me in a net of color and WONDER during the Spring of Discovery are a vestige of what they once were and easily overlooked.

The clutch of confusing fall warblers that offered direct comparison and ushered in the Autumn of Mastery too are a shadow of their former abundance. In fact, I have never again seen so many assembled in the clearing by the lake as I did that day.

And if I were growing up in northern New Jersey today, and there was no Spring of Discovery or Autumn of Mastery, I wonder where else I would have planted the poles that define my life and what sort of life this would have defined.

But a greater part prompts me to wonder what this means to birding's future, if those young people growing up today can find no wonder and will never know mastery.

RIVER DIPPING

We were standing ankle-deep in frost-covered grass. Stripped down to T-shirts and shorts and shivering like poplar trees in a northwest gale. It was first-period gym class, third down, and long yardage (a condition that I have come to regard as a metaphor for my life). Facing off across the line of scrimmage were the fellow members of my high school senior class. On the sidelines, prodding us toward responsible, regimented adulthood, was Good Coach Teddy Bear.

Coach Teddy Bear, who could make a freshman lose bladder control with a glance.

Coach Teddy Bear, whose list of warm-up calisthenics would have exhausted Arnold Schwarzenegger merely to recite.

Coach Teddy Bear, who in the collective memory of Whippany Park High School students was never heard to utter anything more sentimental than "Shower up."

As my classmates took their positions, a sound lofted out of the sky that put the game and all within hearing on hold. It was the sound of geese, one of the most magical sounds on earth, and it was drawing closer.

First one, then another, linebacker, tight end, and offensive lineman (or if you prefer, future accountant, future car salesman, future chemical engineer) stopped what they were doing, straightened, and looked up. In seconds, not a person on the field didn't have his face raised.

It was a large flock, a hundred birds or more, and not very high—not as migrating flocks go. They were close enough to make out the things that birders call field marks, the things that distinguish Canada geese from other geese. But they were distant enough that nothing but our longing could reach them.

One minute passed, two. The sound receded and the great phalanx of birds moved out of sight. Suddenly and simultaneously the chill realization struck.

We'd delayed the game without sanction. We'd courted the wrath of the Teddy Bear and the price would be pain.

Some bravely, some timorously, my classmates and I turned to face our fate—only to discover that the coach seemed oblivious to our indiscretion. In fact, he seemed to have forgotten us. He was still watching the geese, and it seemed to those who stood closest that his eyes were wet.

After another minute, Whippany Park High School's Prince of Pain raised a paw, wiped it across his Marine recruitment poster face, and turned toward the class.

"Wasn't that just too purty?" he said.

It was all we could do to keep from comporting ourselves like freshmen.

I am middle-aged, well-traveled, and fortunate—fortunate to have seen many of the massed bird spectacles the planet has to offer. Flamingo-frosted Lake Borgoria in Kenya, corella clouds at Fog Dam, Australia, snow geese rising off Delaware Bay marshes like an ascending avalanche of white-hot sound.

But the greatest spectacles of all, the ones that mark my past and draw my future, are the ones that take *mass,* add *movement,* and divide it with a *horizon* line. Above all the things that I love about birds, I love migration best.

It's not just numbers because, as I have said, I've seen numbers. They are awe-inspiring, but they are not alluring.

It's not just movement either. I marvel at the falcon's flight and the sympatric precision of shorebird flocks. But I am not captivated. I know what tricks lie hidden beneath the magician's cape.

But when birds rise into the sky and set off to vault hemispheres, something rises in me. I do not know what it is. I scarcely know how to describe it. But I am confident my regard is shared and universal. Why? Two reasons.

First, because there are in this world birders, and I submit that without migration there would be no birders as we know them. There would be ornithologists, who study birds as a scientific endeavor. There would be backyard birdwatchers whose interest in aviforms might be likened to avian landscaping. There just wouldn't be questing, limit-pushing birders.

Quest, after all, needs more than objective: it needs gratification. If every walk through the woods reaped the same rewards (robin, towhee, chickadee) and offered no greater prize or promise (*Connecticut warbler!!!*), quest would have quit, enthusiasm would have succumbed, to ennui long before anyone's interest was piqued. What drives birders to grab binoculars and vault outdoors is the possibility of finding something new.

Migration rolls the dice.

My second reason for believing that migration enjoys near universal allure? Look, if migrating birds can wring rapport out of the impassive likes of Coach Teddy Bear, they can strum a responsive chord in any soul. Including *mine*.

Including *yours*. Go ahead. Look back. Do an accounting of your own great encounters with birds. Not just the exciting ones. Not just the "Oh boy! There it is!" ones. The great ones. I'll bet you'll find, as I did, that most fit the migratory equation: *mass* plus *movement* divided by the *horizon*.

It was binoculars and a book given to a friend in the summer of 1958 that oriented me toward birds—and made catbirds and cardinals the focus of my life. But it was a flood of migrants in the spring of 1962 that put me in touch with a world of color and song and made me aware of possibilities undreamed of.

I was oarless and rudderless in the fall of 1975. And then one day I watched as a river of raptors flowed by. On that day, my life found mooring on a stony hilltop above Kempton, Pennsylvania. A place called Hawk Mountain.

Among the things I love most in this world are fallouts in May;

waves of sharp-shinned hawks pulsing through trees in October; shorebird clouds rising, circling, and setting off toward the Arctic; and the yelp of thrushes on moonless nights.

The most desperate escape I ever witnessed involved a southbound sharp-shinned hawk. The bird was caught offshore, forced to run a gauntlet of herring and black-backed gulls from the horizon to the beach—and it won.

The greatest predator-prey encounter also involved a migrating sharp-shinned hawk. The bird was flying down the tree line north of the hawk watch platform at Cape May Point when it was blindsided by a peregrine, who ferried it from the world of the living to the world of the dead but no further. A northern harrier was on the falcon immediately. The surprised falcon released the sharpie right into the harrier's waiting talons.

Perhaps the most startling act of retaliation I ever witnessed involved a migrating bird and a migrating insect, a monarch butterfly. The young kingbird made a sortie in the insect's direction, snapped, missed, and returned to its perch. The butterfly doubled back and made repeated stoops on the kingbird's head—forcing the young tyrant flycatcher to duck each time.

But without question, the most moving thing I have ever witnessed involved an evening at Cape May Point and a host of migrating passerines. As evening darkened, a host of birds began rising out of the woods and fields of Cape May Point. First there were hundreds, then thousands—robins, waxwings, sparrows, hermit thrushes, and other late-season migrants. They poured from the trees in such numbers that it seemed the woodlands must deflate, and as they climbed they called, filling the air with the calls birds use to encourage each other across the long, dark miles.

It must take great courage to be a bird or it must take great faith, but whichever it is I have taken this moment and others to heart.

There was a Greek philosopher named Heraclitus who once observed that one can put one's foot in a river only once. His point being that a river is constantly changing, never the same, one moment to the next. And he was right.

He had a student who, in the spirit of student trying to outdo the master, carried Heraclitus' observation one step farther. He, the student, said one could not put one's foot in the river even once, because the very act altered the river. He was right too, but he missed something.

People who place themselves in the river's flow not only change the river, they change themselves. As I have changed. As you have changed. As we continue to change. We who stand on the bank of the great north-south river of birds, waiting to see what the next moment brings.